GW00480815

LOW CARB HIGH PROTEIN COOKBOOK

300+ Exciting Low-Carb and High-Protein Recipes for the Art of Healthy Cooking and Weight Management and Optimal Health

By

Lirreyi E. Franks

TABLE OF CONTENT

INTRODUCTION 6

CHAPTER 1: 7

WHAT IS A DIET LOW IN CARBS AND HIGH IN PROTEIN? 7

    BENEFIT 8

CHAPTER 2 11

RECIPE FOR BREAKFAST 11

    GREEK OMELETTE WITH SPINACH AND FETA: 11
    CRUSTLESS QUICHE LORRAINE: 12
    SMOKED SALMON AND AVOCADO LETTUCE WRAPS: 13
    KETO PANCAKES WITH ALMOND FLOUR: 13
    VEGGIE EGG SCRAMBLE WITH TURKEY SAUSAGE: 14
    CHIA SEED PUDDING WITH ALMOND MILK: 15
    COTTAGE CHEESE AND FLAXSEED BOWL: 16
    CAULIFLOWER HASH BROWNS WITH POACHED EGGS: 17
    PROTEIN-PACKED GREEK YOGURT PARFAIT: 18
    BROCCOLI AND CHEDDAR EGG MUFFINS: 19
    CHICKEN AND SPINACH EGG WHITE FRITTATA: 20
    PROSCIUTTO-WRAPPED ASPARAGUS WITH SOFT-BOILED EGGS: 21
    NUTTY COCONUT GRANOLA WITH SEEDS: 22
    SHAKSHUKA WITH GROUND TURKEY 23
    TOFU SCRAMBLE WITH FRESH HERBS 24
    STRAWBERRY AND ALMOND PROTEIN SMOOTHIE 25
    BLUEBERRY AND WALNUT OVERNIGHT PROTEIN OATS 25
    SPICY SAUSAGE AND KALE BREAKFAST SKILLET 26
    ZUCCHINI AND GOAT CHEESE FRITTATA 27
    AVOCADO, BACON, AND EGG BREAKFAST SALAD 28
    SPINACH AND MUSHROOM STUFFED OMELETTE 29
    LOW-CARB ALMOND FLOUR CREPES 30
    TURKEY BACON AND AVOCADO BREAKFAST SANDWICH (LETTUCE WRAP) 31
    SMOKED SALMON AND CREAM CHEESE OMELETTE 32
    COCONUT MILK CHIA PUDDING WITH BERRIES 33
    KETO ALMOND BUTTER GRANOLA BARS 34
    LOW-CARB EGG AND SAUSAGE BURRITO BOWL 35
    MEDITERRANEAN SCRAMBLED EGGS WITH OLIVES AND FETA 36
    BREAKFAST STUFFED BELL PEPPERS 37
    GREEN SMOOTHIE BOWL WITH HEMP SEEDS AND SPINACH 38

CHAPTER 3:RECIPE FOR LUNCH 39

Grilled Chicken Salad with Avocado 39

Greek Salad with Grilled Shrimp 40

Egg Salad Lettuce Wraps 41

Spicy Tuna Salad-Stuffed Avocado 42

Chicken Fajita Bowls 43

Zucchini Noodles with Turkey Meatballs 44

Cauliflower Fried Rice with Chicken 45

Balsamic-Glazed Salmon and Asparagus..46

Chicken and Vegetable Stir-Fry 47

Turkey and Spinach-Stuffed Bell Peppers 48

Cabbage Roll Soup..49

Buffalo Chicken Stuffed Mushrooms 50

Grilled Veggie and Halloumi Skewers 51

Caprese Chicken Lettuce Wraps 52

Chicken Broccoli Alfredo Casserole 53

Asian Chopped Salad with Sesame-Ginger Dressing 54

Shrimp and Avocado Salad 55

Grilled Portobello Mushroom Burgers 56

Lemon Herb Chicken and Vegetable Foil Packets..57

Chicken Shawarma Salad..58

Thai Chicken Lettuce Cups 59

Turkey Taco Salad 61

Zucchini Lasagna Rolls 62

Spinach and Feta Stuffed Chicken Breasts 64

Italian Chopped Salad with Grilled Chicken: 65

Cobb Salad Lettuce Wraps: 66

Quinoa, Black Bean, and Avocado Salad..67

Chicken and Avocado Soup 68

Italian Antipasto Salad 69

Chicken Caesar Collard Green Wraps 70

Roasted Red Pepper and Mozzarella Stuffed Chicken 71

Tofu and Vegetable Stir-Fry 72

Greek Stuffed Peppers...73

Chicken and Spinach Curry...74

Salmon Nicoise Salad 75

Cauliflower Tabouli with Grilled Chicken 76

Turkey Club Lettuce Wraps 77

Mediterranean Chickpea Salad 78

Roasted Veggie Quinoa Salad 79

Chicken and Avocado Caprese Salad 80

Grilled Steak Salad with Blue Cheese 81

Cucumber, Tomato, and Feta Salad 82

Asian Chicken Salad with Peanut Dressing 83

Chicken and Veggie Kabobs 84

SPICY TURKEY AND CAULIFLOWER RICE BOWL 85
GRILLED LEMON HERB TUNA STEAKS 86
CHICKEN AND BLACK BEAN-STUFFED PEPPERS 87
KETO EGG ROLL IN A BOWL...88
CAULIFLOWER HUMMUS WITH VEGGIE STICKS..89
TOFU SCRAMBLE BREAKFAST BURRITO 90

CHAPTER 4: RECIPE FOR DINNER **91**

GRILLED CHICKEN AND AVOCADO SALSA..91
BEEF AND BROCCOLI STIR-FRY 92
ZUCCHINI NOODLES WITH PESTO AND GRILLED CHICKEN 93
LEMON-GARLIC SHRIMP AND ASPARAGUS 94
SEARED AHI TUNA SALAD 95
TURKEY ZUCCHINI MEATBALLS...96
CREAMY TUSCAN CHICKEN SKILLET 97
BLACKENED SALMON WITH AVOCADO SALSA 98
CHICKEN FAJITA STUFFED PEPPERS 99
GARLIC BUTTER BAKED COD 100
KETO CHILI WITH CAULIFLOWER RICE..101
SPINACH AND FETA STUFFED PORK CHOPS 102
ROSEMARY DIJON LAMB CHOPS 103
TURKEY MEATLOAF WITH ROASTED VEGETABLES 104
SHRIMP AND CAULIFLOWER GRITS...105
EGGPLANT ROLLATINI 106
CHICKEN AND MUSHROOM SKILLET WITH CREAM SAUCE 108
ITALIAN SAUSAGE AND KALE SOUP 109
BAKED CHICKEN AND VEGETABLE FOIL PACKETS 110
SPAGHETTI SQUASH CARBONARA 111
GRILLED FLANK STEAK WITH CHIMICHURRI SAUCE 112
PESTO CHICKEN-STUFFED PORTOBELLO MUSHROOMS 113
STUFFED BELL PEPPERS WITH GROUND TURKEY AND CAULIFLOWER RICE 114
CHICKEN PICCATA WITH ZUCCHINI NOODLES 115
BACON-WRAPPED SCALLOPS WITH ASPARAGUS...117
GREEK CHICKEN WITH ROASTED VEGETABLES 118
SALMON AND SPINACH QUICHE 119
SPICY SHRIMP AND ZUCCHINI NOODLES...120
ASIAN BEEF LETTUCE WRAPS 121
CHICKEN CORDON BLEU CASSEROLE 122
BAKED LEMON HERB COD WITH GREEN BEANS 123
GRILLED EGGPLANT PARMESAN 124
CAULIFLOWER PIZZA WITH CHICKEN AND PESTO...125
SKILLET PORK CHOPS WITH CABBAGE AND APPLES..126
STUFFED TOMATOES WITH GROUND CHICKEN AND SPINACH 127
STEAK AND VEGGIE STIR-FRY...128

BAKED GREEK-STYLE SHRIMP WITH TOMATOES AND FETA 129

CHICKEN AND GREEN BEAN STIR-FRY..130

MOROCCAN CHICKEN WITH CAULIFLOWER COUSCOUS 131

SAUSAGE, KALE, AND CAULIFLOWER SOUP...133

CHICKEN, BACON, AND AVOCADO SALAD WITH CREAMY DRESSING 134

LEMON HERB BAKED HALIBUT...135

SPAGHETTI SQUASH AND MEAT SAUCE 136

LOW-CARB CHICKEN POT PIE...137

TOFU AND VEGETABLE CURRY 139

BAKED CHICKEN PARMESAN WITH ZUCCHINI NOODLES..140

SHRIMP AND BROCCOLI ALFREDO..142

GRILLED TOFU WITH CHIMICHURRI SAUCE 143

CHICKEN AND ASPARAGUS SHEET PAN DINNER 144

CAULIFLOWER STEAKS WITH MUSHROOM GRAVY 145

CHAPTER 5:RECIPE FOR SNACKS 147

CAPRESE SALAD SKEWERS...147

PARMESAN CRISPS WITH PROSCIUTTO AND BASIL..147

GREEK SALAD CUCUMBER BITES 148

SPICED MIXED NUTS...149

DEVILED EGGS WITH SMOKED SALMON 150

TUNA-STUFFED MINI BELL PEPPERS 151

CELERY STICKS WITH ALMOND BUTTER..151

TURKEY AND CHEESE ROLL-UPS 152

CHEDDAR AND CHIVE CAULIFLOWER BITES 152

ZUCCHINI PIZZA BITES 153

HAM AND CREAM CHEESE CUCUMBER ROLL-UPS 154

COTTAGE CHEESE WITH BERRIES AND NUTS 154

EDAMAME WITH SEA SALT AND LEMON 155

ROASTED CHICKPEAS WITH GARLIC AND PARMESAN 155

MINI CRUSTLESS QUICHE MUFFINS 156

SPICY ROASTED PUMPKIN SEEDS...157

AVOCADO AND CRAB SALAD-STUFFED ENDIVE...158

BAKED KALE CHIPS WITH NUTRITIONAL YEAST 159

PROSCIUTTO-WRAPPED ASPARAGUS 160

MARINATED MOZZARELLA, CHERRY TOMATOES, AND OLIVES SKEWERS..........................160

CONCLUSION 161

INTRODUCTION

Thank you for choosing this book. "High protein/low carb Cookbook: The kitchen is where 70% of the work is done!" Consume food to maintain health, get in shape, burn fat, and gain muscle. Do you want to get thinner? Some of you would not want to be characterized as "desperate," but do you constantly feel the urge to trim your waistline? I'm positive you do. We know how unpleasant it may be to have trouble sticking to a diet. Not a piece of cake. These fad diets do make you stop eating, which is scary. How long can you maintain calorie counting at each meal? No one, I'm sure, wants to continue doing this. But what about a diet where there are no calorie restrictions? You can start losing weight right now with the low-carb/high-protein diet without taking any medicines, monitoring calories, getting surgery, or experiencing hunger. You'll merely eat some actual food. There are about 20 new, simple low-carb recipes in this book.

The recipes in this book are well explained and broken down step by step. These dishes are divided into two categories: those high in protein and those low in carbohydrates. straightforward, common ingredients that are straightforward to locate at the supermarket are called for in the recipes. You can alter the recipes to suit your preferences, but be careful to limit your intake of carbohydrates. We also noted some of the most significant advantages of a high-protein, low-carb diet. Here is a diet that works and is simple to follow. If you follow this diet exactly, you will experience many advantages. Enjoy your reading!

CHAPTER 1:
WHAT IS A DIET LOW IN CARBS AND HIGH IN PROTEIN?

Low-carb, high-protein diets can help you lose weight and enhance your health by decreasing the amount of carbohydrates you consume. These foods often have more protein, allowing you to gain muscle and reduce fat. While following this diet, you cannot consume processed foods, including chips, sugar, pasta, bread, or even bread. You do not need to give up eating your favorite foods. It advises consuming whole-grain products like pasta, bread, and noodles. On a diet substantial in protein and low in carbohydrates, you can also destroy the following foods:

- Any meat, such as beef, lamb, pork, or chicken. Try to buy as much grass-fed meat as you can.
- All different kinds of fish, like mackerel, salmon, and herring.
- Eggs
- Butter, cream, olive oil, and even coconut oil are all examples of natural fats.
- Cauliflower, mushrooms, cucumbers, Brussels sprouts, collards, kale, Bok Choy, zucchini, and avocado are all vegetables that grow above the ground.
- Dairy products
- All nuts
- Seeds
- Legumes

Any carbs are not considered low carb.

One of the most pervasive misunderstandings is that a low-carb diet excludes all carbohydrates. Carbs included in vegetables, entire fruits, legumes, nuts, whole grains, and seeds are included in the low-carb diet. According to studies, our bodies don't require carbohydrates, but that doesn't mean they aren't beneficial to us. You get energy from carbohydrates, aiding digestion and weight loss. However, consuming too many carbohydrates can cause your metabolism to slow down and cause fatigue. You must pick foods that are high in fiber. Choose starch sources such as sweet potatoes, potatoes, oats, and non-gluten grains instead of pasta, bread, and other foods manufactured with refined flour. You will consume fewer unprocessed carbohydrates if you appropriately implement the low-carb diet. You will find it simple to lose those additional pounds as a result.

BENEFIT

lowered appetites for food and reduced hunger

Two of the main reasons why people struggle to maintain a diet are the discomfort of hunger and the craving for foods high in calories. Low-carb meals address these issues and make it simpler to follow this diet. Conversely, protein aids in releasing hormones that make you feel full in the gut. Consequently, you feel fuller more quickly than if you had simply had a large amount of carbohydrates. You won't ever feel hungry on this diet, and you'll be less tempted to eat a lot of junk food. If you eat fewer carbohydrates, the digestive hormone insulin may also decrease. Your craving for sweet foods will consequently naturally decrease.

There is no requirement to keep track of calories.

You don't need to monitor your calorie intake like other diets. According to studies, those who follow a low-carb, high-protein diet typically consume less food since they can eat as much as they want. People who follow diets that limit their caloric intake frequently experience constant hunger, contributing to weight gain.

Instantaneous weight loss to improve mood

Most people who begin this strategy are eager to lose additional weight. They lose hope and cannot persevere without seeing results immediately. Low-carb diets are fantastic for those who want to start seeing results immediately. People who adhere to this dietary strategy begin to observe developments in just one week.

Your metabolic rate gradually rises as you burn more and more fat. You will succeed in the long term if your digestive system functions.

Gain muscular mass by being thin.

Protein-rich diets aid in fat loss and muscle preservation. Other diets may assist in fat loss but can cause significant muscle strength loss. Your metabolism slows down, and your skin may even start to sag. This diet is unique from all the others in that it enables you to maintain your muscle mass while burning fat. On this diet, you'll consume a lot of fish, eggs, and meat, all high in animal protein. The best protein is found in these natural sources, aiding muscle growth.

Lowers the risk of heart disease and blood pressure

Eating a lot of protein may improve your blood vessels' function and gas release. On the other hand, the low-carb component of this diet plan enhances insulin function. Both of these contribute to maintaining stable blood pressure. Most Americans consume a lot of processed and junk food each day. Thus, this diet might significantly improve their quality of life.

Because of this, most of us have high cholesterol issues, increasing our risk of developing cardiac problems. The low-carb diet lowers insulin levels and cholesterol and guards against diseases like diabetes and heart disease.

In addition to these crucial advantages, the high-protein, low-carb diet has the following benefits:

- Easy-to-follow diet
- Helps you stay satiated
- Repairs hair, skin, and muscle
- Boost energy levels
- Reduction in water retention
- Inexpensive

CHAPTER 2
RECIPE FOR BREAKFAST

GREEK OMELETTE WITH SPINACH AND FETA:

Ingredients:
- 4 large eggs
- 1 cup fresh spinach, chopped
- 1/4 cup crumbled feta cheese
- 2 tablespoons chopped fresh dill
- Salt and pepper, to taste
- 1 tablespoon olive oil

Instructions:
1. In a mixing basin, beat the eggs thoroughly.
2. Combine the beaten eggs with the chopped spinach, feta cheese, dill, salt, and pepper. Blend thoroughly.
3. In a nonstick skillet, heat the olive oil over medium heat.
4. Add the egg mixture and spread it evenly in the skillet.
5. Cook for 3 to 4 minutes or until the bottom is lightly brown and the edges are set.
6. Carefully flip the omelet with a spatula so the other side cooks for 2-3 minutes.
7. When the omelet is fully cooked, place it on a serving platter.
8. Slice and serve hot as a delectable omelet in the Greek style.

CRUSTLESS QUICHE LORRAINE:

Ingredients:
- 6 large eggs
- 1 cup milk
- 1 cup shredded Gruyere or Swiss cheese
- 1/2 cup cooked bacon, crumbled
- 1/2 cup chopped onions
- 1/4 teaspoon salt
- 1/4 teaspoon black pepper
- 1/4 teaspoon dried thyme

Instructions:
1. Set the oven's temperature to 375°F (190°C).
2. In a mixing dish, thoroughly combine the milk and eggs.
3. Add the shredded cheese, cooked bacon, finely chopped onions, salt, black pepper, and dried thyme to the egg mixture. All the components should be mixed.
4. Grease a quiche pan or a 9-inch pie plate.
5. Evenly distribute the contents in the oiled dish after pouring the egg mixture.
6. Bake the dish in the oven for 30-35 minutes or until the quiche is golden brown on top and firm in the center.
7. Take it out of the oven, let it cool, and then slice and serve.
8. Delight in the delicious and flavorful Crustless Quiche Lorraine during breakfast, brunch, or any other time.

SMOKED SALMON AND AVOCADO LETTUCE WRAPS:

Ingredients:
- 4 large lettuce leaves (such as butter lettuce or romaine)
- 4 oz smoked salmon slices
- 1 ripe avocado, sliced
- 1/4 red onion, thinly sliced
- 2 tablespoons capers
- Fresh dill for garnish
- Lemon wedges for serving

Instructions:
1. Place the flattened lettuce leaves on a serving tray after washing and drying them.
2. Arrange a few smoked salmon pieces on top of each lettuce leaf.
3. Add a garnish of avocado, red onion, and capers to the salmon.
4. Add fresh dill as a garnish.
5. Arrange lemon wedges on the side and serve the lettuce wraps.
6. To eat, enclose the fillings in lettuce leaves and savor the tangy flavors.

KETO PANCAKES WITH ALMOND FLOUR:

Ingredients:
- 1 cup almond flour
- 2 tablespoons coconut flour
- 1/2 teaspoon baking powder
- 1/4 teaspoon salt
- 4 large eggs
- 1/4 cup unsweetened almond milk (or any other non-dairy milk)

- 2 tablespoons melted coconut oil (or butter)
- 1 teaspoon vanilla extract
- Optional: sweetener of your choice (such as stevia or erythritol)

Instructions:

1. In a mixing bowl, stir the baking powder, salt, almond flour, and coconut flour.
2. Beat the eggs in a separate basin. Add the vanilla essence, melted coconut oil, almond milk, and sweetener (if using) after that. Mix thoroughly.
3. Mix the dry ingredients thoroughly after adding the wet components. Allowing the batter to settle will help it thicken.
4. Preheat a grill or nonstick skillet over medium heat.
5. For each pancake, spoon about 1/4 cup of the pancake batter into the skillet.
6. Cook for two to three minutes or until surface bubbles appear and the edges begin to set.
7. After flipping the pancakes, fry the opposite side for 1-2 minutes or until golden brown.
8. Carry on by using the leftover batter.
9. Top the warm keto pancakes with your preferred sugar-free syrup or garnishes.

VEGGIE EGG SCRAMBLE WITH TURKEY SAUSAGE:

Ingredients:
- 4 large eggs
- 1/4 cup diced bell peppers (any color)
- 1/4 cup diced onions
- 1/4 cup diced mushrooms
- 2 turkey sausage links, cooked and diced
- Salt and pepper, to taste
- 1 tablespoon olive oil or cooking oil of your choice

- Optional: shredded cheese, fresh herbs (such as parsley or chives) for garnish

Instructions:

1. Beat the eggs and season them with salt and pepper in a bowl. Place aside.
2. In a nonstick skillet over medium heat, warm the olive oil.
3. In the skillet, include the mushrooms, onions, and bell peppers in diced form. Vegetables should be sautéed for 3–4 minutes until they soften.
4. Stir in the diced turkey sausage to the skillet and heat it for 2 minutes.
5. Add the beaten eggs to the skillet of sausage and vegetables.
6. Continue cooking and stirring the eggs until they are scrambled and cooked to the desired doneness.
7. Turn off the heat.
8. If wanted, garnish with shredded cheese and fresh herbs.
9. Serve the vegetable egg scramble hot as a tasty and wholesome option for breakfast or brunch. You can have it by itself, with toast or fresh fruit.

CHIA SEED PUDDING WITH ALMOND MILK:

Ingredients:
- 1/4 cup chia seeds
- 1 cup almond milk (unsweetened)
- 1-2 tablespoons honey or maple syrup (optional for sweetness)
- 1/2 teaspoon vanilla extract
- Fresh fruits or toppings of your choice (such as berries, sliced bananas, chopped nuts, or coconut flakes)

Instructions:

1. Chia seeds, almond milk, honey or maple syrup (if used), and vanilla essence should all be combined in a bowl.

2. Give the mixture a good stir to ensure the chia seeds are dispersed evenly.
3. Stir the mixture once more to avoid clumping after letting it sit for about 5 minutes.
4. Cover the bowl and place the chia seeds in the refrigerator for at least 4 hours or overnight to let the chia seeds absorb the liquid and thicken.
5. Give the pudding a good stir after it has attained the required consistency.
6. Place your preferred fruits or garnishes on the chia seed pudding before serving in dishes or jars.
7. Enjoy the chia seed pudding as a beautiful and healthful breakfast or snack.

COTTAGE CHEESE AND FLAXSEED BOWL:

Ingredients:
- 1 cup cottage cheese
- 2 tablespoons ground flaxseeds
- 1/2 cup fresh berries (such as blueberries, strawberries, or raspberries)
- 1 tablespoon honey or maple syrup (optional for sweetness)
- Chopped nuts or seeds for garnish (optional)

Instructions:
1. Combine cottage cheese and ground flaxseeds in a bowl.
2. Combine thoroughly until the cottage cheese is thoroughly coated with flaxseeds.
3. Add honey or maple syrup to the mixture to add sweetness.
4. Pour in fresh berries and stir them gently into the cottage cheese mixture.
5. Add chopped nuts or seeds on top for flavor and texture.
6. Immediately serve the cottage cheese and flaxseed bowl, or chill until ready to eat.
7. This filling bowl is perfect for breakfast or a snack.

CAULIFLOWER HASH BROWNS WITH POACHED EGGS:

Ingredients:
- 2 cups grated cauliflower
- 1/4 cup grated onion
- 1/4 cup grated Parmesan cheese
- 1/4 cup almond flour
- 2 eggs
- 1/2 teaspoon garlic powder
- 1/2 teaspoon paprika
- Salt and pepper to taste
- Cooking oil or butter for frying
- 4 poached eggs (for serving)
- Fresh parsley or chives for garnish (optional)

Instructions:
1. Mix the grated cauliflower and onion in a big bowl with the Parmesan cheese, almond flour, eggs, garlic powder, paprika, salt, and pepper. To thoroughly incorporate all ingredients, stir well.
2. In a skillet, heat butter or cooking oil over medium heat.
3. Form a patty out of a spoonful of the cauliflower mixture. With a spatula, place the cake in the skillet and flatten it. Make more patties by repeating the process with the leftover mix.
4. Cook the cauliflower hash browns on each side for 3 to 4 minutes or until crispy and golden brown.
5. After cooking, place the hash browns on a platter covered with paper towels to soak up any extra oil.
6. Poach the eggs any way you want them in a different pot.
7. Arrange the poached eggs on top of the cauliflower hash browns. If desired, garnish with fresh chives or parsley.
8. Enjoy the freshly poached eggs with these delectable and healthy hash browns.

PROTEIN-PACKED GREEK YOGURT PARFAIT:

Ingredients:
- 1 cup Greek yogurt
- 1/4 cup granola
- 1/4 cup mixed nuts (such as almonds, walnuts, or cashews), chopped
- 1/4 cup fresh berries (such as blueberries, strawberries, or raspberries)
- 1 tablespoon honey or maple syrup (optional for sweetness)

Instructions:
1. Start piling the ingredients in a glass or bowl.
2. To start, spread Greek yogurt on the bottom.
3. Top the yogurt with a layer of granola.
4. Add a layer of fresh berries, then a layer of mixed nuts.
5. Continue layering until all ingredients have been used, or the desired amount has been attained.
6. To add sweetness, sprinkle honey or maple syrup on top.
7. Immediately serve the Greek yogurt parfait, or chill until ready to eat.
8. This protein-rich parfait makes a pleasant and wholesome breakfast or light snack alternative.

BROCCOLI AND CHEDDAR EGG MUFFINS:

Ingredients:
- 6 large eggs
- 1 cup chopped broccoli florets
- 1/2 cup shredded cheddar cheese
- 1/4 cup diced onion
- 1/4 cup diced bell pepper
- Salt and pepper to taste
- Cooking spray or oil for greasing

Instructions:
1. Set your oven's temperature to 350°F (175°C) and spray or oil a muffin pan.
2. In a mixing bowl, blend the eggs thoroughly.
3. Fill the bowl with the chopped broccoli, crumbled cheddar cheese, onion, and bell pepper. To equally distribute each item, stir well.
4. To taste, add salt and pepper to the dish.
5. Fill each cup in the muffin tin that has been prepared, approximately three-quarters full, with the egg mixture.
6. Bake the egg muffins in the oven for 20 to 25 minutes or until they are set and just beginning to turn golden.
7. After baking the egg muffins, take the muffin tray out of the oven and let it cool.
8. Carefully take the muffins out of the pan and serve them hot. Additionally, they may be chilled for later consumption.
9. These egg muffins with broccoli and cheddar are a tasty and practical breakfast or snack option.

CHICKEN AND SPINACH EGG WHITE FRITTATA:

Ingredients:
- 6 egg whites
- 1 cup cooked chicken breast, shredded or diced
- 1 cup fresh spinach leaves, roughly chopped
- 1/2 cup diced bell pepper
- 1/4 cup diced onion
- 1 clove garlic, minced
- 1/4 teaspoon dried thyme
- Salt and pepper to taste
- Cooking spray or oil for greasing

Instructions:
1. Grease a circular baking dish or pie plate with cooking spray or oil and preheat your oven to 375°F (190°C).
2. Whip the egg whites in a mixing bowl until foamy.
3. Place the cooked chicken breast in the bowl with the spinach, bell pepper, onion, chopped garlic, dry thyme, salt, and pepper. To thoroughly incorporate all ingredients, stir well.
4. Evenly distribute the egg white mixture after pouring it into the prepared baking dish.
5. Bake the frittata in the oven for 20 to 25 minutes or until it is firm and lightly brown.
6. After the frittata has finished cooking, take it from the oven and let it cool.
7. Serve the frittata warm after cutting it into wedges.
8. A light dinner, brunch, or breakfast dish, this chicken and spinach egg white frittata is nutritious and protein-rich.

PROSCIUTTO-WRAPPED ASPARAGUS WITH SOFT-BOILED EGGS:

Ingredients:
- 12 asparagus spears, woody ends trimmed
- 6 slices of prosciutto
- 4 large eggs
- Salt and pepper to taste
- Olive oil for drizzling

Instructions:
1. Set your oven to 400 degrees Fahrenheit (200 degrees Celsius) and cover a baking sheet with parchment paper.
2. Separate the asparagus into 6 bundles, each containing 2 spears.
3. A slice of prosciutto should be securely wrapped around each bundle to enclose the asparagus thoroughly.
4. Set the baked sheet with the wrapped asparagus bundles on it.
5. Bake for 10 to 12 minutes or until the prosciutto is crisp and the asparagus is soft.
6. Prepare the soft-boiled eggs while the asparagus is baking. Water should be added to a saucepan and brought to a boil. For soft-boiled eggs, add the eggs and simmer for around 6 minutes.
7. To halt the cooking of the eggs, remove them from the boiling water and place them in a dish of icy water. After a short cooling period, carefully peel the shells off.
8. Add salt and pepper to taste and season the eggs.
9. After the prosciutto-wrapped asparagus is finished cooking, lay it on a platter with a soft-boiled egg next to it.
10. Drizzle with olive oil and, if preferred, add more salt and pepper.
11. Soft-boiled eggs and the prosciutto-wrapped asparagus make a delicious and beautiful brunch or breakfast dish.

NUTTY COCONUT GRANOLA WITH SEEDS:

Ingredients:
- 2 cups rolled oats
- 1/2 cup unsweetened shredded coconut
- 1/2 cup mixed nuts (such as almonds, walnuts, or pecans), chopped
- 1/4 cup pumpkin seeds
- 1/4 cup sunflower seeds
- 1/4 cup honey or maple syrup
- 2 tablespoons coconut oil, melted
- 1/2 teaspoon vanilla extract
- 1/4 teaspoon cinnamon (optional)
- Pinch of salt

Instructions:
1. Set a baking sheet on your oven's 325°F (165°C) rack and preheat the oven.
2. Combine the rolled oats, coconut shreds, mixed nuts, pumpkin seeds, sunflower seeds, salt, and cinnamon in a large bowl.
3. Combine the vanilla extract, melted coconut oil, and honey or maple syrup in a different small dish.
4. Fill the large bowl with the dry ingredients and top with the liquid mixture. To ensure that all the dry ingredients are coated, thoroughly stir the mixture.
5. Evenly spread the granola mixture onto the baking sheet that has been prepared.
6. Bake the granola in the preheated oven for 25 to 30 minutes, stirring halfway through or until it is crisp and golden brown.
7. Take the baking sheet out of the oven and let the granola cool.
8. After it has cooled, put the granola in an airtight container to keep it fresh.

9. Use the crisp and flavorful nutty coconut granola with seeds as a garnish over smoothie bowls or yogurt, or eat it as a snack.

SHAKSHUKA WITH GROUND TURKEY

Ingredients:
- 1 tablespoon olive oil
- 1 onion, diced
- 2 cloves garlic, minced
- 1 bell pepper, diced
- 1 pound ground turkey
- 1 teaspoon ground cumin
- 1 teaspoon ground paprika
- 1/2 teaspoon ground cayenne pepper (adjust to taste)
- 1 can (14 ounces) crushed tomatoes
- Salt and pepper to taste
- 4-6 large eggs
- Fresh parsley, chopped (for garnish)

Instructions:
1. Heat olive oil in a large skillet or frying pan over medium heat.
2. Add the diced onion, minced garlic, and bell pepper to the pan. Sauté until the vegetables are softened and slightly caramelized.
3. Add the ground turkey to the pan and cook until it is browned and cooked, breaking it into smaller pieces with a spoon or spatula.
4. Stir in the ground cumin, paprika, and ground cayenne pepper, and cook for 1-2 minutes to toast the spices.
5. Pour in the crushed tomatoes and stir well. Reduce the heat to low and let the mixture simmer for 10-15 minutes to allow the flavors to meld together. Season with salt and pepper to taste.
6. Create small wells in the tomato mixture and carefully crack the eggs into each well. Cover the pan and let the

eggs cook until the whites are set but the yolks are still slightly runny about 5-7 minutes.
7. Garnish with fresh parsley and serve the shakshuka hot with crusty bread or pita on the side.

TOFU SCRAMBLE WITH FRESH HERBS

Ingredients:
- 1 tablespoon olive oil
- 1 small onion, diced
- 2 cloves garlic, minced
- 1 bell pepper, diced
- 1 block (14 ounces) of firm tofu, drained and crumbled
- 2 tablespoons nutritional yeast
- 1 teaspoon ground turmeric
- 1/2 teaspoon ground cumin
- Salt and pepper to taste
- 2 tablespoons fresh herbs (such as parsley, basil, or chives), chopped

Instructions:

1. Heat the olive oil over medium heat in a big frying pan or skillet.
2. Include the bell pepper, onion, and garlic in the pan. Sauté the vegetables until they are tender and beginning to caramelize.
3. Add the crushed tofu to the pan and simmer, stirring for about 5 minutes.
4. Add salt, pepper, nutritional yeast, turmeric, and cumin, for the tofu to absorb the spices and the flavors to meld; simmer for 3 to 4 minutes.
5. Stirring often, add the fresh herbs, and simmer for 1-2 minutes.
6. Taste and, if necessary, adjust the seasoning.
7. Take the tofu scramble off the fire and serve it hot. It can be done alone or with tortillas, toast, or any other side dish you choose.

STRAWBERRY AND ALMOND PROTEIN SMOOTHIE

Ingredients:
- 1 cup frozen strawberries
- 1 ripe banana
- 1 cup almond milk (or any milk of your choice)
- 1 scoop vanilla protein powder
- 1 tablespoon almond butter
- 1 tablespoon honey or maple syrup (optional for added sweetness)
- Ice cubes (optional)

Instructions:
1. Blend the almond milk, vanilla protein powder, almond butter, frozen strawberries, ripe banana, and honey or maple syrup (if using) in a blender.
2. Until the smoothie is creamy and all the ingredients are thoroughly blended, blend on high speed.
3. Add a few ice cubes and blend until smooth if you prefer a cooler and thicker smoothie.
4. After tasting the smoothie, add honey or maple syrup if necessary to increase its sweetness.
5. Pour the smoothie into a glass and consume it immediately for a cool, protein-rich beverage.

BLUEBERRY AND WALNUT OVERNIGHT PROTEIN OATS

Ingredients:
- 1/2 cup rolled oats
- 1/2 cup milk (dairy or plant-based)
- 1/2 cup Greek yogurt
- 1 tablespoon chia seeds
- 1 tablespoon maple syrup or honey

- 1/4 teaspoon vanilla extract
- 1/4 cup fresh or frozen blueberries
- 2 tablespoons chopped walnuts

Instructions:

1. Combine the rolled oats, milk, Greek yogurt, chia seeds, maple syrup or honey, and vanilla extract in a jar or other container with a tight-fitting lid.
2. Make sure all the ingredients are well combined by vigorously stirring.
3. Gently incorporate the blueberries and walnut halves.
4. To help the oats soften and take in the flavors, cover the jar or container and place it in the refrigerator overnight or at least 4-6 hours.
5. Stir the oats thoroughly in the morning and consume them warm or cold straight from the jar, depending on your preference.
6. Before serving, you can top the dish with more blueberries, walnuts, or honey.

SPICY SAUSAGE AND KALE BREAKFAST SKILLET

Ingredients:
- 1 tablespoon olive oil
- 1 pound spicy sausage, casings removed
- 1 onion, diced
- 2 cloves garlic, minced
- 1 bell pepper, diced
- 2 cups kale, stems removed and leaves chopped
- Salt and pepper to taste
- 4-6 eggs

Instructions:

1. Heat the olive oil over medium heat in a big frying pan or skillet.

2. When the spicy sausage is ready, add it to the pan and cook it, breaking it up with a spoon or spatula as it cooks.
3. Include the bell pepper, onion, and garlic in the pan. Sauté the vegetables until they are tender and beginning to caramelize.
4. Add the chopped kale and stir; cook until wilted and soft.
5. To taste, add salt and pepper to the food.
6. Make a few little wells in the skillet and carefully crack the eggs into each well. Cover the pan and boil the eggs for about 5-7 minutes, or until the whites are set but the yolks are still a little runny.
7. Remove the breakfast skillet from the heat and serve it hot, placing an egg on each serving.

ZUCCHINI AND GOAT CHEESE FRITTATA

Ingredients:
- 1 tablespoon olive oil
- 1 zucchini, thinly sliced
- 1/2 onion, thinly sliced
- 6 large eggs
- 1/4 cup milk
- Salt and pepper to taste
- 2 ounces goat cheese, crumbled
- Fresh basil leaves, torn (for garnish)

Instructions:
1. Set the oven's temperature to 350°F (175°C).
2. Heat the olive oil in a skillet that can be used in a range.
3. Add the onion and zucchini slices to the skillet and cook until they are tender and beginning to caramelize.
4. Thoroughly blend the eggs, milk, salt, and pepper in a bowl.
5. Spoon the egg mixture into the skillet, covering the onion and zucchini equally.
6. Sprinkle goat cheese crumbles on top of the frittata.

7. On the burner, cook the frittata for 2 to 3 minutes or until the edges begin to set.
8. Place the pan in the hot oven, and bake for 15 to 20 minutes until the frittata is set and the top turns golden.
9. Take it out of the range, then give it some time to cool.
10. Add shredded basil leaves as a garnish.
11. Serve the frittata warm or at room temperature after cutting it into wedges.

AVOCADO, BACON, AND EGG BREAKFAST SALAD

Ingredients:
- 4 cups mixed greens (such as lettuce, spinach, or arugula)
- 4 slices bacon, cooked and crumbled
- 2 hard-boiled eggs, sliced
- 1 avocado, sliced
- 1/2 cup cherry tomatoes, halved
- 1/4 cup red onion, thinly sliced
- 2 tablespoons chopped fresh herbs (such as parsley or chives)
- Salt and pepper to taste
- Dressing of your choice (such as balsamic vinaigrette or lemon vinaigrette)

Instructions:
1. Combine the mixed greens, crumbled bacon, sliced hard-boiled eggs, cherry tomatoes, red onion, and finely chopped fresh herbs in a large salad bowl.
2. To taste, add salt and pepper to the food.
3. Pour your preferred salad dressing over the contents and gently toss to coat.
4. Immediately serve the avocado, bacon, and egg breakfast salad as a filling and healthy breakfast option.

SPINACH AND MUSHROOM STUFFED OMELETTE

Ingredients:
- 3 large eggs
- 1 tablespoon milk
- Salt and pepper to taste
- 1 tablespoon butter
- 1 cup fresh spinach leaves
- 1/2 cup sliced mushrooms
- 1/4 cup shredded cheese (such as cheddar or feta)
- Fresh herbs (such as parsley or chives) for garnish

Instructions:
1. Thoroughly blend the eggs, milk, salt, and pepper in a bowl.
2. Melt and warm the butter in a nonstick skillet over medium heat.
3. Add the spinach to the skillet along with the thinly sliced mushrooms, and cook until the spinach wilts and the mushrooms soften.
4. Cover the spinach and mushrooms with an equal layer of the egg mixture in the skillet.
5. After a few minutes of cooking the omelet, tilt the skillet and gently lift the edges with a spatula to let the uncooked egg flow to the edges.
6. Evenly cover one-half of the omelet with the shredded cheese.
7. Fold the second half of the omelet using a spatula over the cheese side.
8. Continue cooking for one more minute or until the cheese is melted and the omelet is done.
9. Transfer the omelet to a platter and add fresh herbs as a garnish.
10. Present the hot spinach and mushroom omelet with bread or fresh fruit on the side.

LOW-CARB ALMOND FLOUR CREPES

Ingredients:
- 1 cup almond flour
- 2 tablespoons coconut flour
- 4 large eggs
- 1/2 cup unsweetened almond milk (or any milk of your choice)
- 1/4 teaspoon salt
- 1/2 teaspoon vanilla extract
- Cooking spray or butter for greasing the pan

Instructions:

1. In a mixing bowl, combine the eggs, almond milk, salt, vanilla essence, and almond flour until a homogeneous mixture develops.
2. Let the batter sit for 5 to 10 minutes to let the coconut flour absorb the liquid.
3. Lightly spray or butter a nonstick skillet or crepe pan with cooking spray before heating it.
4. Swirl the batter in the pan to distribute it into a thin, even layer. Pour about 1/4 cup of the batter into the pan.
5. Cook the crepe for 2 to 3 minutes or until the center is set and the sides are golden brown.
6. Carefully flip the crepe over using a spatula, and cook on the other side for 1-2 minutes
7. Please take out the cooked crepe and set it aside.
8. Continue until all of the crepes are cooked using the remaining batter.
9. Top the crepes made with almond flour with your favorite contents, such as Greek yogurt, fresh fruit, or a thin layer of sugar-free syrup.

TURKEY BACON AND AVOCADO BREAKFAST SANDWICH (LETTUCE WRAP)

Ingredients:
- 4 large lettuce leaves (such as romaine or butter lettuce)
- 4 slices of turkey bacon
- 2 large eggs
- Salt and pepper to taste
- 1 ripe avocado, sliced
- Tomato slices (optional)
- Mayonnaise or your preferred condiment (optional)

Instructions:
1. In a skillet over medium heat, toast up the turkey bacon. Take out of the skillet, then set it aside.
2. Prepare the eggs in the same skillet as you choose (fried, scrambled, or poached). Add salt and pepper to taste.
3. Top a lettuce leaf with a cooked egg, a piece of turkey bacon, avocado, and tomato slices (if using).
4. If desired, top with a dab of mayonnaise or another sauce.
5. To make a lettuce wrap, fold the lettuce leaf over the filling.
6. Carry out the procedure once again using the leftover lettuce leaves and ingredients.
7. Immediately serve the turkey bacon and avocado breakfast sandwiches and savor the light and low-carb take on a traditional breakfast sandwich.

SMOKED SALMON AND CREAM CHEESE OMELETTE

Ingredients:
- 3 large eggs
- Salt and pepper to taste
- 1 tablespoon butter or oil
- 2 ounces smoked salmon, thinly sliced
- 2 tablespoons cream cheese, softened
- Fresh dill, chopped (for garnish)

Instructions:
1. In a bowl, beat the eggs, salt, and pepper until well combined.
2. Melt and warm the butter or oil in a nonstick skillet over medium heat.
3. After adding the beaten eggs to the skillet, turn it to spread the mixture evenly.
4. After a few minutes, cook the omelet until the edges firm.
5. Arrange the smoked salmon pieces and softened cream cheese on one half of the omelet once it has set chiefly but is still somewhat runny on top.
6. Gently fold the remaining omelet in half over the filling.
7. Cook for a further minute or until the omelet is done and the cream cheese has softened.
8. Place the hot omelet on a platter and top with fresh dill.

COCONUT MILK CHIA PUDDING WITH BERRIES

Ingredients:
- 1/4 cup chia seeds
- 1 cup coconut milk (canned or carton)
- 1 tablespoon maple syrup or honey
- 1/2 teaspoon vanilla extract
- Fresh berries (such as strawberries, blueberries, or raspberries) for topping

Instructions:

1. Combine the chia seeds, coconut milk, maple syrup or honey, and vanilla essence in a bowl or container. To blend, thoroughly stir.
2. Give the mixture a second toss after 5 minutes to stop the chia seeds from clumping together.
3. To allow the chia seeds to absorb the liquid and develop a pudding-like consistency, cover the bowl or jar and place it in the refrigerator for at least 4 hours or overnight.
4. Stir the chia pudding thoroughly to remove any clumps before serving.
5. Distribute the chia pudding among serving glasses or bowls.
6. Add toppings, such as shredded coconut or finely chopped nuts, and fresh berries.
7. Serve the cooled coconut milk chia pudding and savor a rich and wholesome breakfast.

KETO ALMOND BUTTER GRANOLA BARS

Ingredients:
- 1 cup almond butter
- 1/4 cup coconut oil
- 1/4 cup low-carb sweetener (such as erythritol or stevia)
- 1 teaspoon vanilla extract
- 1/2 teaspoon cinnamon
- 2 cups mixed nuts and seeds (such as almonds, walnuts, pecans, sunflower seeds, and chia seeds)
- 1/4 cup unsweetened shredded coconut
- 1/4 cup sugar-free chocolate chips (optional)

Instructions:

1. Combine the almond butter, coconut oil, low-carb sweetener, vanilla extract, and cinnamon in a saucepan over low heat.
2. Place the shredded coconut, mixed nuts and seeds, and sugar-free chocolate chips (if using) in a large bowl.
3. Pour the melted combination of almond butter over the dry ingredients, then stir to combine.
4. Parchment paper to line a baking dish and firmly press the mixture onto the plate to make an equal layer.
5. Place the container in the refrigerator for at least two hours to make the granola bars solid and set.
6. After they have dried, cut the bars off the plate into bars or squares of the required size.
7. You can keep the almond butter granola bars in the fridge for up to a week by placing them in an airtight container.

LOW-CARB EGG AND SAUSAGE BURRITO BOWL

Ingredients:
- 4 large eggs
- Salt and pepper to taste
- 4 ounces cooked sausage, crumbled
- 1/4 cup diced bell peppers
- 1/4 cup diced onion
- 1/4 cup shredded cheddar cheese
- 1/4 cup salsa
- Optional toppings: avocado slices, sour cream, chopped cilantro

Instructions:
1. Beat the eggs in a basin and season with salt and pepper.
2. Lightly drizzle oil or cook with cooking spray in a nonstick skillet heated to medium heat.
3. Add the diced onions and bell peppers to the skillet and cook until tender.
4. Pour the whisked eggs into one side of the skillet and push the sautéed vegetables to the other.
5. Continue scrambling the eggs until they reach the desired doneness.
6. Combine the eggs and vegetables in the skillet with the crumbled sausage.
7. Top the mixture with crumbled cheddar cheese and allow it to melt.
8. Switch off the heat and pour the egg and sausage mixture into a bowl.
9. If desired, add salsa and any other garnishes, like avocado slices, sour cream, or chopped cilantro.
10. Savor the hearty and tasty low-carb egg and sausage burrito dish for breakfast.

MEDITERRANEAN SCRAMBLED EGGS WITH OLIVES AND FETA

Ingredients:
- 4 large eggs
- 2 tablespoons milk
- Salt and pepper to taste
- 2 tablespoons olive oil
- 1/4 cup diced red onion
- 1/4 cup diced tomatoes
- 1/4 cup sliced Kalamata olives
- 1/4 cup crumbled feta cheese
- Fresh parsley, chopped (for garnish)

Instructions:
1. Thoroughly blend the eggs, milk, salt, and pepper in a bowl.
2. In a nonstick skillet over medium heat, warm the olive oil.
3. Stir in the diced red onion and cook for three to five minutes or until tender.
4. Stir in the diced tomatoes and Kalamata olives, and cook for a few minutes until the tomatoes soften.
5. When the eggs are scrambled and cooked to the correct consistency, pour the egg mixture into the skillet and stir gently.
6. Top the scrambled eggs with the crumbled feta cheese and mix to combine.
7. Turn off the heat and add some fresh parsley as a garnish.
8. Immediately serve the hot Mediterranean scrambled eggs with toast or a choice of side.

BREAKFAST STUFFED BELL PEPPERS

Ingredients:
- 4 bell peppers (any color)
- 4 large eggs
- Salt and pepper to taste
- 1/4 cup diced cooked bacon or sausage (optional)
- 1/4 cup diced tomatoes
- 1/4 cup shredded cheddar cheese
- Fresh parsley or chives, chopped (for garnish)

Instructions:
1. Set the oven's temperature to 375°F (190°C).
2. Cut the bell peppers in half and remove the membranes and seeds.
3. Arrange the bell peppers upright in a baking dish.
4. Fill each bell pepper with an egg. Add salt and pepper to taste.
5. Top each bell pepper with shredded cheddar cheese, sliced tomatoes, and optional cooked bacon or sausage.
6. Bake the eggs in the oven for 20 to 25 minutes, depending on how you like your eggs.
7. Take them out of the range, then give them time to cool.
8. Add fresh chives or parsley as a garnish.
9. Warm up the bell peppers and serve them with the breakfast.

GREEN SMOOTHIE BOWL WITH HEMP SEEDS AND SPINACH

Ingredients:
- 1 ripe banana, frozen
- 1 cup spinach leaves
- 1/2 cup unsweetened almond milk (or any milk of your choice)
- 1 tablespoon almond butter
- 1 tablespoon hemp seeds
- Toppings: sliced fresh fruit, granola, additional hemp seeds

Instructions:
1. Combine the frozen banana, hemp seeds, spinach leaves, almond milk, and almond butter in a blender.
2. Blend on high power until creamy and smooth. If more almond milk is required, add it until the desired consistency is reached.
3. Fill a bowl with the green smoothie.
4. Add granola, hemp seeds, and sliced fresh fruit over the top for more flavor and texture.
5. Use a spoon to devour the green smoothie bowl immediately.

CHAPTER 3:
RECIPE FOR LUNCH

GRILLED CHICKEN SALAD WITH AVOCADO

Ingredients:
- 2 boneless, skinless chicken breasts
- Salt and pepper to taste
- 1 tablespoon olive oil
- 4 cups mixed salad greens
- 1 avocado, sliced
- 1 cup cherry tomatoes, halved
- 1/4 cup red onion, thinly sliced
- 1/4 cup sliced cucumber
- 1/4 cup crumbled feta cheese
- 2 tablespoons chopped fresh herbs (such as parsley or basil)
- Lemon wedges (for serving)

For the dressing:

- 2 tablespoons extra-virgin olive oil
- 1 tablespoon lemon juice
- 1 clove garlic, minced
- Salt and pepper to taste

Instructions:
1. Set a grill or grill pan to medium-high heat in step 1.
2. Rub some olive oil, salt, and pepper on the chicken breasts.
3. Grill the chicken for 6 to 8 minutes on each side or until it is fully cooked and reaches a temperature of 165°F (74°C).
4. Take the chicken off the grill and let it rest for a while. Make thin strips out of it.

5. Combine the mixed salad greens, avocado slices, cherry tomatoes, red onion, thinly sliced cucumber, and crumbled feta cheese in a sizable salad bowl.
6. Combine the extra virgin olive oil, lemon juice, minced garlic, salt, and pepper in a small bowl to make the dressing.
7. Pour the sauce over the salad and gently toss to distribute the contents evenly.
8. Include grilled chicken slices in the salad, along with some fresh herbs.
9. To add even more flavor, serve the grilled chicken salad with wedges of avocado and lemon.

GREEK SALAD WITH GRILLED SHRIMP

Ingredients:
- 1 pound large shrimp, peeled and deveined
- Salt and pepper to taste
- 1 tablespoon olive oil
- 4 cups chopped romaine lettuce
- 1 cup cherry tomatoes, halved
- 1/2 cucumber, diced
- 1/4 cup sliced red onion
- 1/4 cup Kalamata olives
- 1/4 cup crumbled feta cheese
- Fresh dill or parsley, chopped (for garnish)

For the dressing:

- 2 tablespoons extra-virgin olive oil
- 1 tablespoon red wine vinegar
- 1 clove garlic, minced
- 1/2 teaspoon dried oregano
- Salt and pepper to taste

Instructions:
1. Set a grill or grill pan to medium-high heat in step 1.

2. Add olive oil, salt, and pepper to the shrimp.
3. Grill the shrimp for two to three minutes on each side or until pink and fully cooked.
4. After taking the shrimp off the grill, set them aside.
5. Combine the Kalamata olives, chopped romaine lettuce, cherry tomatoes, diced cucumber, sliced red onion, and crumbled feta cheese in a sizable salad bowl.
6. To make the dressing, combine the extra virgin olive oil, red wine vinegar, minced garlic, dried oregano, salt, and pepper in a small bowl.
7. Pour the salad dressing over it and gently mix the items to coat them all.
8. Include the shrimp in the salad and some fresh dill or parsley as a garnish.
9. Grilled shrimp with Greek salad provide a tasty and energizing lunch.

EGG SALAD LETTUCE WRAPS

Ingredients:
- 6 hard-boiled eggs, peeled and chopped
- 1/4 cup mayonnaise
- 1 tablespoon Dijon mustard
- 2 tablespoons finely chopped celery
- 2 tablespoons finely chopped red onion
- 1 tablespoon chopped fresh dill (optional)
- Salt and pepper to taste
- Lettuce leaves (such as butter lettuce or romaine) for wrapping

Instructions:

1. Combine the celery, red onion, chopped hard-boiled eggs, mayonnaise, Dijon mustard, and fresh dill (if using) in a bowl. Blend thoroughly.
2. Add salt and pepper to taste and, if needed, modify the amount of mayonnaise and mustard.

3. Scoop a small amount of egg salad into the center of each lettuce leaf.
4. When enclosing the egg salad with a lettuce leaf, use toothpicks to keep it in place.
5. Carry out step 5 with the rest of the lettuce leaves and egg salad.
6. Offer the lettuce wraps stuffed with egg salad as a lite, protein-rich lunch or snack.

SPICY TUNA SALAD-STUFFED AVOCADO

Ingredients:
- 2 cans (5 ounces each) of tuna, drained
- 1/4 cup mayonnaise
- 1 tablespoon Sriracha sauce (adjust to taste)
- 1 tablespoon lime juice
- 2 green onions, thinly sliced
- Salt and pepper to taste
- 2 ripe avocados
- Fresh cilantro leaves (for garnish)

Instructions:
1. In a bowl, combine the tuna that has been drained, mayonnaise, Sriracha sauce, lime juice, and green onions. Blend thoroughly.
2. To taste, add salt and pepper and more or less Sriracha sauce to achieve the appropriate heat level.
3. Halve the avocados and scoop out the pits.
4. Scoop a little flesh from the center of each avocado half to make room for the tuna salad.
5. Fill the avocado halves to the brim with the spicy tuna salad.
6. Add fresh cilantro leaves as a garnish.
7. As a tasty and filling lunch, serve the avocados stuffed with spicy tuna salad.

CHICKEN FAJITA BOWLS

Ingredients: For the chicken marinade:
- 1 pound boneless, skinless chicken breasts, thinly sliced
- 2 tablespoons olive oil
- 2 tablespoons lime juice
- 1 teaspoon chili powder
- 1 teaspoon ground cumin
- 1 teaspoon paprika
- 1/2 teaspoon garlic powder
- Salt and pepper to taste

For the fajita bowls:

- 2 tablespoons olive oil
- 1 bell pepper, thinly sliced
- 1 onion, thinly sliced
- Salt and pepper to taste
- Lettuce or cooked rice as the base
- Toppings: avocado slices, salsa, shredded cheese, sour cream, cilantro (optional)

Instructions:

1. To make the marinade, mix the olive oil, lime juice, chili powder, cumin powder, paprika, garlic powder, salt, and pepper in a bowl.
2. Add the marinade to the chicken slices, thoroughly covering it. Give 30 minutes to marinate or overnight in the fridge for additional flavor.
3. Place a sizable skillet or pan over medium-high heat and add 1 tablespoon olive oil.
4. Add the marinated chicken to the skillet and cook for 6 to 8 minutes or until thoroughly done. Place aside.
5. Heat a further tablespoon of olive oil in the same skillet, then add the bell pepper and onion slices. Cook for about 5 to 6 minutes or until they are softened and start caramelizing. Add salt and pepper to taste.

6. To assemble your fajita bowls, start with a foundation of lettuce or cooked rice, then add the cooked chicken, bell pepper, onion, and any additional toppings you choose, such as salsa, shredded cheese, sour cream, cilantro, or avocado slices.
7. Dish out the chicken fajita bowls and take a bite.

ZUCCHINI NOODLES WITH TURKEY MEATBALLS

Ingredients: For the turkey meatballs:
- 1 pound ground turkey
- 1/4 cup almond flour
- 1/4 cup grated Parmesan cheese
- 1/4 cup chopped fresh parsley
- 1 clove garlic, minced
- 1/2 teaspoon dried oregano
- 1/2 teaspoon dried basil
- Salt and pepper to taste
- 1 large egg, beaten

For the zucchini noodles:

- 4 medium zucchini, spiralized
- 2 tablespoons olive oil
- 2 cloves garlic, minced
- Salt and pepper to taste
- Grated Parmesan cheese (for garnish)

Instructions:

1. Mix the ground turkey, almond flour, grated Parmesan cheese, fresh parsley that has been chopped, minced garlic, dried oregano, dried basil, salt, pepper, and the beaten egg in a large basin. Blend thoroughly.
2. Form the turkey mixture into little meatballs with a diameter of 1 inch.

3. Place a sizable skillet or pan over medium heat and add 1 tablespoon olive oil. Add the turkey meatballs and simmer for 8 to 10 minutes or until thoroughly cooked. Place aside.
4. Heat a further tablespoon of olive oil in the same skillet, then add the minced garlic. Cook until aromatic for approximately 1 minute.
5. Stir in the spiralized zucchini noodles and simmer for 2 to 3 minutes or until they soften. Add salt and pepper to taste.
6. Arrange the turkey meatballs on top of the zucchini noodles on the dishes.
7. Add grated Parmesan cheese as a garnish.
8. Arrange the turkey meatballs on top of the zucchini noodles, and savor!

CAULIFLOWER FRIED RICE WITH CHICKEN

Ingredients:
- 1 head cauliflower, riced (or use pre-riced cauliflower)
- 2 tablespoons sesame oil (or olive oil)
- 2 boneless, skinless chicken breasts, diced
- 1 small onion, diced
- 2 cloves garlic, minced
- 1 cup mixed vegetables (such as peas, carrots, and corn)
- 2 tablespoons soy sauce (or tamari for gluten-free)
- 1 tablespoon oyster sauce (optional)
- 2 green onions, sliced
- Salt and pepper to taste
- Sesame seeds (for garnish)

Instructions:
1. Heat 1 tablespoon of sesame oil to medium heat in a big skillet or wok.
2. Add the chicken dice to the skillet and heat until it is browned. The chicken should be taken out of the skillet and put aside.

3. Add the remaining tablespoon of sesame oil in the same skillet and cook the minced garlic and diced onion until aromatic.
4. Add the mixed vegetables to the skillet and heat them for a few minutes.
5. Slide the veggies to one side of the skillet and top with the baked cauliflower.
6. Cook the cauliflower for 5 to 6 minutes, tossing once or twice or until it's done and just beginning to turn brown.
7. Add the cooked chicken to the skillet and combine it with the vegetables and cauliflower.
8. Add the soy sauce and oyster sauce (if using) and toss everything together thoroughly to cover everything.
9. To taste, add salt and pepper to the dish.
10. Add sesame seeds and thinly sliced green onions as a garnish.
11. Present the chicken and cauliflower fried rice hot and savor!

BALSAMIC-GLAZED SALMON AND ASPARAGUS

Ingredients:
- 4 salmon fillets
- Salt and pepper to taste
- 1 bunch asparagus, ends trimmed
- 2 tablespoons olive oil
- 3 tablespoons balsamic vinegar
- 2 tablespoons honey (or maple syrup for a vegan option)
- 2 cloves garlic, minced
- Fresh parsley or basil, chopped (for garnish)

Instructions:
1. Set the oven's temperature to 400°F (200°C).
2. Add salt and pepper to the salmon fillets.

3. Spread 1 tablespoon of olive oil on a baking pan and add the asparagus. Add salt and pepper to taste.
4. Combine the balsamic vinegar, honey, minced garlic, and a last tablespoon of olive oil in a separate bowl.
5. Arrange the salmon fillets and the asparagus on the baking sheet.
6. Drizzle the salmon with the balsamic glaze mixture and toss the asparagus to coat it.
7. Bake the salmon and asparagus in the oven for 12 to 15 minutes, depending on how you want your salmon.
8. Remove from the oven, then top with basil or fresh parsley.
9. Present the wild asparagus and fish with balsamic glaze.

CHICKEN AND VEGETABLE STIR-FRY

Ingredients:
- 2 boneless, skinless chicken breasts, thinly sliced
- Salt and pepper to taste
- 2 tablespoons soy sauce
- 1 tablespoon oyster sauce (optional)
- 1 tablespoon cornstarch
- 2 tablespoons vegetable oil
- 2 cloves garlic, minced
- 1 tablespoon grated ginger
- 1 bell pepper, thinly sliced
- 1 carrot, thinly sliced
- 1 cup broccoli florets
- 1 cup snap peas or snow peas
- 2 green onions, sliced
- Sesame seeds (for garnish)

Instructions:
1. In a bowl, combine the salt, pepper, soy sauce, oyster sauce (if using), and cornstarch with the sliced chicken

breasts. To evenly coat the chicken, thoroughly mix. Allow to marinate for approximately 10 minutes.
2. Heat the vegetable oil over medium-high heat in a sizable skillet or wok.
3. Add the grated ginger and minced garlic to the skillet and cook for approximately a minute or until fragrant.
4. Add the chicken that has been marinating to the skillet and cook it through with continuous stirring.
5. Fill the skillet with the sliced bell pepper, carrot, broccoli florets, and snap peas. Cook for 3 to 4 minutes or until the vegetables are crisp.
6. Add the green onions, stir, and cook for one more minute.
7. Taste the dish and, if necessary, add more salt, pepper, or soy sauce to the seasoning.
8. Add sesame seeds as a garnish.
9. Hot stir-fry with chicken and vegetables should be served with steamed rice or noodles.

TURKEY AND SPINACH-STUFFED BELL PEPPERS

Ingredients:
- 4 bell peppers (any color), tops removed and seeds removed
- 1 pound ground turkey
- 1 small onion, diced
- 2 cloves garlic, minced
- 1 cup baby spinach, chopped
- 1 cup cooked quinoa or rice
- 1/4 cup grated Parmesan cheese
- 1 teaspoon dried oregano
- Salt and pepper to taste
- 1/2 cup shredded mozzarella cheese

Instructions:
1. Set the oven's temperature to 375°F (190°C).

2. Brown the ground turkey in a large skillet over medium heat. Remove any extra fat.
3. Stir in the minced garlic and onion and cook until the onion is transparent.
4. Add the spinach and sauté it in the skillet until it wilts.
5. Combine the quinoa or rice cooked with the grated Parmesan cheese, salt, pepper, and dried oregano. Blend thoroughly.
6. Stuff the turkey and spinach mixture into each bell pepper.
7. Spread the shredded mozzarella cheese over the filled bell peppers in a baking dish.
8. Bake in the oven for 25 to 30 minutes or until the cheese is brown and the bell peppers are soft.
9. Take them out of the range and allow them to cool before serving.
10. Serve the filled bell peppers hot with turkey and spinach.

CABBAGE ROLL SOUP

Ingredients:
- 1 pound ground beef
- 1 onion, diced
- 3 cloves garlic, minced
- 4 cups beef broth
- 1 can (14.5 ounces) diced tomatoes
- 1 can (8 ounces) tomato sauce
- 1/2 cup uncooked rice
- 1/2 head cabbage, chopped
- 1 teaspoon dried oregano
- 1 teaspoon dried basil
- Salt and pepper to taste
- Fresh parsley, chopped (for garnish)

Instructions:
1. Brown the ground beef in a big Dutch oven or pot over medium heat. Remove any extra fat.

2. Stir in the minced garlic and onion, and cook until the onion is transparent.
3. Add salt, pepper, dried oregano, dried basil, diced tomatoes, tomato sauce, uncooked rice, chopped cabbage, and beef broth.
4. After bringing the mixture to a boil, lower the heat and simmer it for 20 to 25 minutes, or until the rice and cabbage are done and soft.
5. Taste and, if necessary, adjust the seasoning.
6. Garnish the hot cabbage roll soup with fresh parsley.

BUFFALO CHICKEN STUFFED MUSHROOMS

Ingredients:
- 12 large mushrooms, stems removed
- 1 cup cooked chicken, shredded or diced
- 1/4 cup buffalo sauce
- 4 ounces cream cheese, softened
- 1/4 cup shredded cheddar cheese
- 2 green onions, sliced
- Salt and pepper to taste
- Ranch or blue cheese dressing (for dipping)

Instructions:
1. Preheat your oven to 375°F (190°C).
2. In a bowl, combine the cooked chicken, buffalo sauce, cream cheese, cheddar cheese that has been shredded, green onion slices, salt, and pepper. Blend thoroughly.
3. On a baking sheet, arrange the mushroom caps.
4. Generously stuff each mushroom cap with the buffalo-chicken mixture.
5. Bake for 15 to 20 minutes or until the filling is hot and the mushrooms are soft.
6. Take them out of the oven, then give them time to cool.

7. Offer ranch or blue cheese dressing besides the buffalo chicken-stuffed mushrooms for dipping.

GRILLED VEGGIE AND HALLOUMI SKEWERS

Ingredients:
- 8 wooden skewers, soaked in water for 30 minutes
- 8 ounces of halloumi cheese, cut into cubes
- 1 zucchini, sliced into rounds
- 1 yellow bell pepper, cut into chunks
- 1 red onion, cut into chunks
- Cherry tomatoes
- 2 tablespoons olive oil
- 2 tablespoons balsamic vinegar
- 1 teaspoon dried oregano
- Salt and pepper to taste

Instructions:
1. Start your grill or grill pan by heating it to medium-high.
2. Thread the cherry tomatoes, zucchini rounds, red onion, yellow bell pepper chunks, and halloumi cheese onto the moistened wooden skewers.
3. To create the marinade, combine the salt, pepper, dried oregano, olive oil, balsamic vinegar, and salt in a small bowl.
4. Coat the skewers thoroughly with the marinade by brushing it on.
5. After the skewers have been placed on the heated grill, cook them for about 5-7 minutes, turning them once or twice or until the vegetables are soft and the halloumi cheese is just starting to sear.
6. Take the skewers from the grill, then warm them up before serving.

CAPRESE CHICKEN LETTUCE WRAPS

Ingredients:
- 2 boneless, skinless chicken breasts
- Salt and pepper to taste
- 2 tablespoons olive oil
- 4 large lettuce leaves (such as romaine or butter lettuce)
- 4 slices fresh mozzarella cheese
- 2 tomatoes, sliced
- Fresh basil leaves
- Balsamic glaze or reduction (optional)

Instructions:

1. Add salt and pepper to the chicken breasts.
2. In a skillet over medium heat, warm the olive oil.
3. Add the chicken breasts to the skillet and cook for 6 to 8 minutes on each side until the chicken is well cooked and the middle is no longer pink.
4. Take the chicken out of the skillet and let it rest for a while. The chicken should then be cut into tiny strips.
5. After spreading fresh mozzarella cheese on each lettuce leaf, arrange the leaves.
6. Add fresh basil leaves, chicken pieces, and tomato slices on top.
7. If desired, drizzle with balsamic glaze or reduction.
8. To make lettuce wraps, roll up the lettuce leaves.
9. Present the Caprese chicken lettuce wraps as a tasty and light supper.

CHICKEN BROCCOLI ALFREDO CASSEROLE

Ingredients:
- 8 ounces penne pasta
- 2 cups cooked chicken, shredded or diced
- 2 cups broccoli florets
- 2 tablespoons butter
- 2 cloves garlic, minced
- 2 tablespoons all-purpose flour
- 2 cups milk
- 1 cup shredded mozzarella cheese
- 1/2 cup grated Parmesan cheese
- Salt and pepper to taste

Instructions:
1. Set the oven's temperature to 375°F (190°C).
2. Prepare the penne pasta as directed on the package until it is al dente. Drain, then set apart.
3. Melt the butter in a sizable skillet over medium heat. Add the minced garlic and cook for approximately a minute or until fragrant.
4. To produce a roux, stir in the flour and heat for a further minute.
5. Stir in the milk gradually, making sure there are no lumps.
6. Continue cooking the sauce while stirring regularly until it thickens and simmers.
7. Turn off the heat and whisk the grated Parmesan and shredded mozzarella cheese until melted and evenly distributed.
8. To taste, add salt and pepper to the sauce.
9. Mix the penne pasta, chicken, and broccoli florets in a big bowl. Stirring to ensure that everything is equally coated, pour the Alfredo sauce over the mixture.
10. Pour the mixture into a casserole dish that has been buttered.

11. Bake the casserole in the oven for 20 to 25 minutes or until it bubbles.
12. Take it out of the range and allow it to cool before serving.
13. Provide the cozy and filling chicken broccoli Alfredo dish as a dinner.

ASIAN CHOPPED SALAD WITH SESAME-GINGER DRESSING

Ingredients: For the sesame-ginger dressing:
- 2 tablespoons sesame oil
- 2 tablespoons soy sauce
- 1 tablespoon rice vinegar
- 1 tablespoon honey or maple syrup
- 1 teaspoon grated fresh ginger
- 1 clove garlic, minced

For the salad:

- 6 cups mixed salad greens
- 1 cup shredded carrots
- 1 cup thinly sliced cucumber
- 1/2 cup thinly sliced red bell pepper
- 1/2 cup chopped green onions
- 1/4 cup chopped fresh cilantro
- 1/4 cup chopped roasted peanuts or sesame seeds (for garnish)

Instructions:
1. Making the dressing in a small bowl, combine the sesame oil, soy sauce, rice vinegar, honey or maple syrup, grated ginger, and chopped garlic. Place aside.
2. Combine the mixed salad greens, shredded carrots, cucumber slices, red bell pepper slices, chopped green onions, and cilantro in a sizable salad bowl.

3. After drizzling the sesame-ginger dressing over the salad, gently mix the items to evenly distribute it.
4. Add chopped toasted peanuts or sesame seeds as a garnish.
5. Use the Asian chopped salad as a light supper or a tasty side dish.

SHRIMP AND AVOCADO SALAD

Ingredients:
- 1 pound shrimp, peeled and deveined
- Salt and pepper to taste
- 2 tablespoons olive oil
- 4 cups mixed salad greens
- 1 avocado, sliced
- 1 cup cherry tomatoes, halved
- 1/4 cup red onion, thinly sliced
- 1/4 cup chopped fresh cilantro or parsley
- Juice of 1 lime

For the dressing:

- 2 tablespoons extra-virgin olive oil
- 1 tablespoon lime juice
- 1 clove garlic, minced
- Salt and pepper to taste

Instructions:
1. Sprinkle some salt and pepper on the shrimp.
2. In a skillet over medium-high heat, warm the olive oil.
3. Add the shrimp to the skillet and cook them for two to three minutes per side or until they are pink and cooked through.
4. Take the shrimp out of the pan and place them aside.

5. Combine the mixed salad greens, diced avocado, cherry tomatoes, red onion, and chopped cilantro or parsley in a sizable salad bowl.
6. Combine the extra virgin olive oil, lime juice, minced garlic, salt, and pepper in a small bowl to make the dressing.
7. Pour the salad dressing over it and gently mix the items to coat them all.
8. Add the lime juice and cooked shrimp to the salad.
9. Continue tossing to blend.
10. Immediately serve the shrimp and avocado salad.

GRILLED PORTOBELLO MUSHROOM BURGERS

Ingredients:
- 4 large Portobello mushroom caps
- 2 tablespoons balsamic vinegar
- 2 tablespoons soy sauce
- 2 tablespoons olive oil
- 2 cloves garlic, minced
- Salt and pepper to taste
- 4 burger buns or lettuce leaves for wrapping
- Toppings of your choice (such as lettuce, tomato, onion, avocado, and condiments)

Instructions:
1. To create the marinade, combine the balsamic vinegar, soy sauce, olive oil, minced garlic, salt, and pepper in a small bowl.
2. Cut the stems off the Portobello mushroom caps, then brush the marinade on both sides of the lids.
3. Turn on the medium heat for a grill or grill pan.
4. Place the mushroom caps, gill side down, on the heated grill.

5. Grill the mushrooms for 4–5 minutes per side or until they are fork-tender and have grill marks.
6. Take the mushroom caps from the grill and set them aside to cool.
7. Put each Portobello mushroom cap on a bread or lettuce leaf to assemble the grilled burgers.
8. Top with garnishes like lettuce, tomato, onion, avocado, and sauces.
9. Distribute the Portobello mushroom burgers and savor them!

LEMON HERB CHICKEN AND VEGETABLE FOIL PACKETS

Ingredients:
- 4 boneless, skinless chicken breasts
- Salt and pepper to taste
- 2 tablespoons olive oil
- 2 cloves garlic, minced
- 1 teaspoon dried thyme
- 1 teaspoon dried rosemary
- Zest and juice of 1 lemon
- 2 cups mixed vegetables (such as bell peppers, zucchini, and carrots), chopped
- Fresh herbs (such as parsley or basil), chopped (for garnish)

Instructions:
1. Set the oven's temperature to 375°F (190°C).
2. Add salt and pepper to the chicken breasts.
3. To make the marinade, combine the olive oil, minced garlic, rosemary, dried thyme, and lemon juice in a small bowl.
4. Lay out every chicken breast on its piece of aluminum foil.
5. Distribute the mixed veggies among the foil pouches, positioning them close to the chicken.

6. Drizzle the chicken and vegetables with the marinade.
7. Create a packet by folding the foil over the chicken and vegetables and sealing the edges.
8. Arrange the foil packages on a baking sheet and bake for 20 to 25 minutes, or until the chicken is cooked and the vegetables are soft.
9. Transfer the chicken and veggies to serving dishes after carefully opening the foil packs.
10. Add fresh herbs as a garnish.
11. Serve the chicken and vegetables in foil packets with lemon and hot herbs.

CHICKEN SHAWARMA SALAD

Ingredients: For the chicken shawarma:
- 1 pound boneless, skinless chicken thighs or breasts
- 2 tablespoons olive oil
- 2 cloves garlic, minced
- 1 teaspoon ground cumin
- 1 teaspoon ground paprika
- 1/2 teaspoon ground coriander
- 1/2 teaspoon ground turmeric
- 1/4 teaspoon ground cinnamon
- Salt and pepper to taste

For the salad:

- 4 cups mixed salad greens
- 1 cucumber, diced
- 1 tomato, diced
- 1/4 cup red onion, thinly sliced
- 1/4 cup chopped fresh parsley
- 1/4 cup chopped fresh mint
- Juice of 1 lemon
- 2 tablespoons extra-virgin olive oil
- Salt and pepper to taste
- Tahini sauce or garlic sauce (optional for serving)

Instructions:

1. Combine the marinade, salt, pepper, garlic powder, cumin powder, paprika powder, coriander powder, turmeric powder, and cinnamon powder in a bowl with the olive oil.
2. Include the chicken thighs or breasts in the marinade and thoroughly coat them. Give them 30 minutes to marinate or overnight in the fridge for extra flavor.
3. Heat a grill or grill pan to a high temperature.
4. Grill the marinated chicken for 6 to 8 minutes on each side or until it is well cooked and the middle is no longer pink. After removing them from the grill, give them some time to rest.
5. Cut the chicken from the grill into thin strips.
6. Combine the mixed salad greens, diced cucumber, tomato, red onion, thinly sliced fresh parsley, and fresh mint in a large salad bowl.
7. To make the dressing, combine the lemon juice, extra virgin olive oil, salt, and pepper in a small bowl.
8. Pour the salad dressing and gently mix to coat all the ingredients.
9. Include the salad with the chicken shawarma slices.
10. To add flavor, Tahini sauce or garlic sauce can optionally be served on the side with the chicken shawarma salad.

THAI CHICKEN LETTUCE CUPS

Ingredients: For the chicken:
- 1 pound ground chicken
- 2 tablespoons soy sauce
- 2 tablespoons hoisin sauce
- 1 tablespoon fish sauce
- 1 tablespoon lime juice
- 1 tablespoon brown sugar
- 2 cloves garlic, minced
- 1 teaspoon grated fresh ginger

- 1/4 teaspoon red pepper flakes (optional)
- Salt and pepper to taste

For the lettuce cups:

- 8-10 large lettuce leaves (such as butter lettuce or romaine)
- 1/2 cup shredded carrots
- 1/2 cup diced cucumber
- 1/4 cup chopped fresh cilantro
- 1/4 cup chopped fresh mint
- Lime wedges (for serving)

Instructions:

1. To make the marinade, whisk together the soy sauce, hoisin sauce, fish sauce, lime juice, brown sugar, shredded ginger, red pepper flakes (if using), salt, and pepper.
2. Add the marinade to the ground chicken, thoroughly covering it. Allow it to marinade for 15 to 30 minutes.
3. Bring a pan or skillet to medium-high heat. Cook the chicken, breaking it up with a spoon as it cooks, until it is browned and well done.
4. Turn off the heat and allow the cooked chicken cool slightly.
5. To build the cup, pour a portion of the cooked chicken into each lettuce leaf.
6. Add chopped fresh mint, cilantro, diced cucumber, and shredded carrots.
7. Before serving, squeeze a lime wedge over each lettuce cup.
8. Offer Thai chicken lettuce cups as a tasty and healthy starter or main course.

TURKEY TACO SALAD

Ingredients: For the turkey:
- 1 pound ground turkey
- 1 tablespoon olive oil
- 1 small onion, diced
- 2 cloves garlic, minced
- 1 tablespoon chili powder
- 1 teaspoon ground cumin
- 1/2 teaspoon paprika
- Salt and pepper to taste

For the salad:

- 6 cups mixed salad greens
- 1 cup cherry tomatoes, halved
- 1/2 cup diced bell peppers
- 1/2 cup canned black beans, rinsed and drained
- 1/4 cup diced red onion
- 1/4 cup chopped fresh cilantro
- 1/4 cup shredded cheddar cheese (optional)
- Sliced avocado (optional)
- Tortilla chips (optional)

For the dressing:

- 1/4 cup plain Greek yogurt
- 1 tablespoon lime juice
- 1 tablespoon chopped fresh cilantro
- Salt and pepper to taste

Instructions:

1. Heat the olive oil over medium heat in a skillet or other pan. Add the minced garlic and onion, and cook until aromatic and tender.
2. Add the ground turkey to the skillet and heat it, breaking it up as it cooks with a spoon until it is browned and thoroughly cooked.

3. Add the salt, pepper, paprika, cumin powder, and chili powder. To enable the flavors to combine, cook for one more minute. Take it off the fire and give it a minute to cool.
4. Combine the mixed salad greens, cherry tomatoes, bell peppers, black beans, red onion, fresh cilantro, and cheddar cheese (if using) in a large salad bowl.
5. To create the dressing, combine the Greek yogurt, lime juice, finely chopped fresh cilantro, salt, and pepper in a small bowl.
6. Drizzle the salad with the dressing, then gently toss to coat all the ingredients evenly.
7. Place some cooked ground turkey on top of the salad.
8. If preferred, garnish with crumbled tortilla chips and diced avocado.
9. Offer the turkey taco salad as a filling and tasty supper.

ZUCCHINI LASAGNA ROLLS

Ingredients:
- 4 large zucchini
- 1 pound ground beef or turkey
- 1 small onion, diced
- 2 cloves garlic, minced
- 1 can (14 ounces) crushed tomatoes
- 1/2 cup tomato sauce
- 1 teaspoon dried oregano
- 1 teaspoon dried basil
- Salt and pepper to taste
- 1 cup ricotta cheese
- 1/2 cup grated Parmesan cheese
- 1 egg, beaten
- 2 cups shredded mozzarella cheese
- Fresh basil leaves (for garnish)

Instructions:
1. Set the oven's temperature to 375°F (190°C).

2. Cut the zucchini into thin, 1/4-inch-thick strips by slicing it lengthwise.
3. Brown the ground beef or turkey in a large skillet over medium heat. Remove any extra fat.
4. Add the minced garlic and onion to the skillet, and cook until the onion is transparent.
5. Add salt, pepper, dried oregano, dry basil, tomato sauce, and smashed tomatoes. To allow the flavors to mingle, simmer for about 10 minutes. Get rid of the heat.
6. Mix the ricotta cheese, Parmesan cheese, and beaten egg in a medium bowl. Mix thoroughly.
7. Place a ribbon of zucchini on the table and thinly layer the ricotta cheese mixture along its length.
8. Smear a little of the beef sauce on top of the cheese mixture.
9. Place the zucchini strip, seam-side down, in a prepared baking dish after rolling it up.
10. Carry out the same procedure with the remaining filling and zucchini strips.
11. Cover the zucchini rolls with the remaining meat sauce and top with shredded mozzarella cheese.
12. Place foil over the baking dish and bake for about 20 minutes.
13. Take off the foil and bake the cheese for 10-15 minutes or until it is melted and brown.
14. Add fresh basil leaves as a garnish.
15. Warm the zucchini lasagna rolls before serving.

SPINACH AND FETA STUFFED CHICKEN BREASTS

Ingredients:
- 4 boneless, skinless chicken breasts
- Salt and pepper to taste
- 2 cups fresh spinach leaves
- 1/2 cup crumbled feta cheese
- 2 cloves garlic, minced
- 1 tablespoon olive oil
- 1 tablespoon lemon juice
- 1 teaspoon dried oregano
- 1/2 teaspoon paprika
- Toothpicks

Instructions:
1. Set the oven's temperature to 400°F (200°C).
2. Add salt and pepper to the chicken breasts.
3. Heat the olive oil in a skillet over medium heat. Add the minced garlic and cook for approximately a minute or until fragrant.
4. Stir in the fresh spinach leaves and heat in the skillet until they wilt.
5. Turn off the heat and mix the feta cheese crumbles, lemon juice, dry oregano, and paprika. Mix thoroughly.
6. Be cautious not to cut all the way through when creating a pocket in each chicken breast by making a horizontal incision along the side.
7. Gently press the spinach and feta mixture into each chicken breast. Use toothpicks to close the gap.
8. Turn up the heat on a skillet to medium-high. The stuffed chicken breasts should be added and seared for two to three minutes on each side or until golden brown.
9. Place the baked chicken breasts in a preheated oven and bake for 20 to 25 minutes, until the chicken is cooked and no longer pink in the middle.
10. Before serving, take out the toothpicks.

11. Present the chicken breasts with feta and spinach, stuffing hot.

ITALIAN CHOPPED SALAD WITH GRILLED CHICKEN:

Ingredients: For the grilled chicken:
- 2 boneless, skinless chicken breasts
- Salt and pepper to taste
- 1 tablespoon olive oil
- 1 teaspoon dried Italian seasoning

For the salad:

- 6 cups mixed salad greens
- 1 cup cherry tomatoes, halved
- 1 cup diced cucumber
- 1/2 cup diced red bell pepper
- 1/2 cup sliced black olives
- 1/4 cup diced red onion
- 1/4 cup sliced pepperoncini peppers
- 1/4 cup grated Parmesan cheese
- 1/4 cup chopped fresh basil
- 2 tablespoons chopped fresh parsley

For the dressing:

- 3 tablespoons extra-virgin olive oil
- 2 tablespoons red wine vinegar
- 1 clove garlic, minced
- 1 teaspoon Dijon mustard
- Salt and pepper to taste

Instructions:
1. Start your grill or grill pan by heating it to medium-high.
2. Add dried Italian seasoning, salt, and pepper to the chicken breasts.

3. Liberally brush the chicken breasts with olive oil.
4. Place the chicken breasts on the prepared grill and cook for 6 to 8 minutes on each side until the chicken is well cooked and the middle is no longer pink.
5. Take the chicken off the grill and rest for a few minutes. After that, cut them into narrow strips.
6. Place the mixed salad greens, diced cucumber, diced red bell pepper, diced red onion, diced pepperoncini peppers, grated Parmesan cheese, chopped fresh basil, and chopped fresh parsley in a large salad bowl.
7. To make the dressing, combine the extra virgin olive oil, red wine vinegar, garlic powder, Dijon mustard, salt, and pepper in a small bowl.
8. Pour the salad dressing and gently mix to coat all the ingredients.
9. Include the salad with the sliced, grilled chicken.
10. Grilled chicken and the Italian chopped salad make a tasty and filling supper.

COBB SALAD LETTUCE WRAPS:

Ingredients:
- 4 large lettuce leaves (such as romaine or butter lettuce)
- 8 slices cooked bacon, crumbled
- 2 hard-boiled eggs, chopped
- 1 cup cooked chicken breast, diced
- 1 avocado, diced
- 1 cup cherry tomatoes, halved
- 1/2 cup crumbled blue cheese
- 1/4 cup diced red onion
- 1/4 cup chopped fresh parsley
- Salt and pepper to taste
- Ranch dressing (optional for serving)

Instructions:
1. Put the lettuce leaves in a single layer on a plate or serving platter.

2. Arrange the crumbled bacon, diced hard-boiled eggs, cherry tomatoes, chicken breast, avocado, red onion, and chopped fresh parsley in each lettuce leaf.
3. To taste, add salt and pepper to the dish.
4. Drizzle ranch dressing over the toppings, if desired.
5. To make lettuce wraps, carefully wrap each lettuce leaf around the filling.
6. Immediately serve the Cobb Salad Lettuce Wraps.

QUINOA, BLACK BEAN, AND AVOCADO SALAD

Ingredients:
- 1 cup cooked quinoa
- 1 can (15 ounces) of black beans, rinsed and drained
- 1 avocado, diced
- 1 cup cherry tomatoes, halved
- 1/4 cup diced red onion
- 1/4 cup chopped fresh cilantro
- Juice of 1 lime
- 2 tablespoons extra-virgin olive oil
- Salt and pepper to taste

Instructions:

1. Mix the cooked quinoa, black beans, diced avocado, cherry tomatoes, red onion, and fresh cilantro in a big bowl.
2. Combine the lime juice, extra virgin olive oil, salt, and pepper in a small bowl to make the dressing.
3. After adding the sauce to the salad, gently toss the ingredients in the dressing to combine.
4. Offer the salad of quinoa, black beans, and avocado as a tasty, wholesome side dish or quick meal.

CHICKEN AND AVOCADO SOUP

Ingredients:
- 1 tablespoon olive oil
- 1 small onion, diced
- 2 cloves garlic, minced
- 2 medium carrots, diced
- 2 celery stalks, diced
- 4 cups chicken broth
- 2 cups cooked chicken, shredded
- 1 avocado, diced
- Juice of 1 lime
- Salt and pepper to taste
- Fresh cilantro (for garnish)

Instructions:

1. In a pot set over medium heat, warm the olive oil. Add the minced garlic and onion, and cook until aromatic and tender.
2. Stir in the diced carrots and celery and simmer for 3 to 4 minutes.
3. Add the chicken broth, then heat it to a boil. The vegetables should be soft after 10 minutes of simmering at a reduced heat.
4. Add the diced avocado and cooked chicken that has been shredded. Five more minutes of simmering.
5. Add the lime juice to the soup and taste-test, adding salt and pepper.
6. Place fresh cilantro on top of the chicken and avocado soup before serving.
7. Hot-serve the soup.

ITALIAN ANTIPASTO SALAD

Ingredients:
- 6 cups mixed salad greens
- 1 cup cherry tomatoes, halved
- 1 cup diced cucumber
- 1 cup diced bell peppers
- 1 cup sliced pepperoni or salami
- 1/2 cup sliced black olives
- 1/2 cup marinated artichoke hearts, drained and chopped
- 1/4 cup diced red onion
- 1/4 cup grated Parmesan cheese
- 1/4 cup chopped fresh basil
- 2 tablespoons red wine vinegar
- 2 tablespoons extra-virgin olive oil
- Salt and pepper to taste

Instructions:
1. Toss the mixed salad greens, cherry tomatoes, diced cucumber, bell peppers, sliced pepperoni or salami, sliced black olives, diced red onion, grated Parmesan cheese, and fresh basil together in a large salad bowl.
2. To make the dressing, combine the extra virgin olive oil, red wine vinegar, salt, and pepper in a small bowl.
3. Pour the sauce over the salad and toss to distribute it over all of the ingredients evenly.
4. Offer the colorful and delectable Italian Antipasto Salad as an appetizer or main entrée.

CHICKEN CAESAR COLLARD GREEN WRAPS

Ingredients:

- 4 large collard green leaves
- 2 cups cooked chicken, shredded or sliced
- 1/4 cup grated Parmesan cheese
- 1/4 cup Caesar dressing
- 1/4 cup croutons (optional)
- Salt and pepper to taste

Instructions:

1. Rinse and dry the collard green leaves.
2. Carefully cut along the side of each collard green leaf to remove the rough stem.
3. Put the cooked chicken with the shredded Parmesan cheese, Caesar dressing, croutons (if using), salt, and pepper in a bowl. Mix thoroughly.
4. Lay a collard leaf out on a spotless surface. Spread a dollop of the chicken mixture equally across the leaf after spooning it on.
5. Form a wrap by tightly rolling the collard green leaf around the filling and tucking the sides in as you move.
6. The remaining collard green leaves and the chicken mixture should be prepared similarly.
7. If desired, cut the wrappers in half. If necessary, fasten with toothpicks.
8. Offer your guests the Chicken Caesar Collard Green Wraps as a filling and healthful lunch or snack.

ROASTED RED PEPPER AND MOZZARELLA STUFFED CHICKEN

Ingredients:
- 4 boneless, skinless chicken breasts
- Salt and pepper to taste
- 4 roasted red peppers, sliced
- 8 slices mozzarella cheese
- 2 tablespoons olive oil
- 2 cloves garlic, minced
- 1 teaspoon dried Italian seasoning

Instructions:
1. Set the oven's temperature to 375°F (190°C).
2. Add salt and pepper to the chicken breasts.
3. Cut a pocket for the stuffing by slicing each chicken breast lengthwise.
4. Insert mozzarella cheese and roasted red pepper slices into each chicken breast.
5. Use toothpicks to close the chicken breasts' openings.
6. In an oven-safe skillet, heat the olive oil over medium-high heat. Italian dried seasoning and minced garlic are added and cooked until aromatic.
7. In a skillet, fry the stuffed chicken breasts for 4-5 minutes on each side or until browned.
8. Place the skillet in the preheated oven, and bake for 15 to 20 minutes until the cheese is melted and bubbling and the chicken is cooked through.
9. Before serving, take out the toothpicks.
10. Present the chicken with roasted red pepper and mozzarella stuffing hot.

TOFU AND VEGETABLE STIR-FRY

Ingredients:

- 14 ounces firm tofu, drained and pressed
- 2 tablespoons soy sauce
- 1 tablespoon sesame oil
- 1 tablespoon cornstarch
- 2 tablespoons vegetable oil
- 2 cloves garlic, minced
- 1 small onion, thinly sliced
- 1 bell pepper, thinly sliced
- 1 cup broccoli florets
- 1 carrot, thinly sliced
- 1 cup snap peas
- 2 tablespoons hoisin sauce
- 1 tablespoon rice vinegar
- 1/2 teaspoon red pepper flakes (optional)
- Salt and pepper to taste
- Cooked rice or noodles (optional for serving)

Instructions:

1. Slice or cube the tofu, then pat it dry with a paper towel.
2. Mix the cornstarch, soy sauce, and sesame oil in a bowl. Mix thoroughly.
3. Include the tofu in the basin and gently toss it around to spread the marinade. Give it around 15 minutes to marinate.
4. Heat the vegetable oil over medium-high heat in a sizable skillet or wok.
5. Place the onion slices in the skillet with the minced garlic and cook until the onion is transparent and the garlic is fragrant.
6. Fill the skillet with the bell pepper, broccoli florets, carrot slices, and snap peas. Cook the vegetables in a stir-fry for 3 to 4 minutes or until they are crisp and tender.

7. Move the vegetables to one side of the skillet and add the tofu that has been marinated to the other. The tofu should be browned and crispy after cooking it for two to three minutes on each side.
8. Combine the hoisin sauce, rice vinegar, and red pepper flakes (if using) in a small bowl. Over the tofu and veggies in the skillet, pour the sauce. Stir to distribute the coating evenly.
9. To taste, add salt and pepper to the dish.
10. Turn off the heat and serve the stir-fry with plain tofu and vegetables or overcooked rice or noodles, if you want.

GREEK STUFFED PEPPERS

Ingredients:
- 4 bell peppers (any color)
- 1 pound ground beef or lamb
- 1 small onion, diced
- 2 cloves garlic, minced
- 1 cup cooked rice (white or brown)
- 1/2 cup crumbled feta cheese
- 1/4 cup chopped Kalamata olives
- 1/4 cup chopped sun-dried tomatoes
- 1 teaspoon dried oregano
- Salt and pepper to taste
- Olive oil (for drizzling)

Instructions:
1. Set the oven's temperature to 375°F (190°C).
2. Cut off the bell peppers' tops, then scoop out the seeds and membranes.
3. Brown the ground beef or lamb in a large skillet over medium heat. Remove any extra fat.
4. Add the minced garlic and onion to the skillet, and cook until the onion is transparent.

5. Combine the feta cheese crumbles, chopped Kalamata olives, sun-dried tomatoes, dried oregano, salt, and pepper with the cooked rice. Mix thoroughly.
6. Gently press the filling mixture into the bell peppers while doing so.
7. Put the peppers in a baking tray after being filled. Add a drizzle of olive oil.
8. Bake for 30-35 minutes or until the filling is heated and the peppers are soft.
9. Take them out of the oven and cool a bit before serving.
10. Make the Greek Stuffed Peppers the centerpiece of a fantastic meal.

CHICKEN AND SPINACH CURRY

Ingredients:
- 1 tablespoon vegetable oil
- 1 onion, finely chopped
- 2 cloves garlic, minced
- 1 tablespoon curry powder
- 1 teaspoon ground cumin
- 1 teaspoon ground coriander
- 1/2 teaspoon turmeric
- 1/4 teaspoon cayenne pepper (optional, adjust to taste)
- 1 pound boneless, skinless chicken breasts cut into cubes
- 1 can (14 ounces) diced tomatoes
- 1 cup coconut milk
- 2 cups fresh spinach leaves
- Salt and pepper to taste
- Cooked rice or naan bread (for serving)

Instructions:
1. Heat the vegetable oil over medium heat in a big skillet or pan.
2. Add the minced garlic and onion to the skillet and cook until the onion is transparent and tender.

3. Add the cayenne pepper (if using), turmeric, ground cumin, ground coriander, and curry powder. Cook until aromatic for approximately 1 minute.
4. Add the chicken cubes to the pan and sauté until evenly browned.
5. Add the coconut milk and diced tomatoes with their juices. To blend, stir.
6. Lower the heat to a low simmer and cook the curry for 15 to 20 minutes or until the chicken is cooked.
7. Add the fresh spinach leaves and stir; simmer for 2–3 minutes or until wilted.
8. To taste, add salt and pepper to the dish.
9. Turn off the heat and allow the curry to cool before serving.
10. Alternatively, serve the Chicken and Spinach Curry with naan bread and boiled rice.

SALMON NICOISE SALAD

Ingredients:
- 4 salmon fillets
- Salt and pepper to taste
- 4 cups mixed salad greens
- 1 cup cherry tomatoes, halved
- 1 cup cooked green beans, cut into bite-sized pieces
- 1/2 cup sliced black olives
- 4 hard-boiled eggs, sliced
- 1/4 cup chopped red onion
- 2 tablespoons capers
- Lemon wedges (for serving)
- For the dressing:
- 1/4 cup extra-virgin olive oil
- 2 tablespoons red wine vinegar
- 1 tablespoon Dijon mustard
- 1 clove garlic, minced
- Salt and pepper to taste

Instructions:

1. Start your grill or grill pan by heating it to medium-high.
2. Add salt and pepper to the salmon fillets.
3. Grill the salmon fillets for four to five minutes on each side or until done and flaky. Remove them from the fire and let them a brief moment to cool.
4. Combine the mixed salad greens, capers, red onion, cherry tomatoes, cooked green beans, sliced black olives, and hard-boiled eggs.
5. In a big salad bowl.
6. To create the dressing, combine the extra virgin olive oil, red wine vinegar, Dijon mustard, garlic powder, salt, and pepper in a small bowl.
7. Pour the salad dressing over it and gently mix the items to coat them all.
8. Slice up the grilled salmon fillets and scatter them over the salad.
9. Put lemon wedges on the side and serve the salmon Nicoise salad.

CAULIFLOWER TABOULI WITH GRILLED CHICKEN

Ingredients:

- 1 small head of cauliflower, cut into florets
- 1 cup cherry tomatoes, halved
- 1/2 cup chopped cucumber
- 1/4 cup chopped red onion
- 1/4 cup chopped fresh parsley
- 2 tablespoons chopped fresh mint
- Juice of 1 lemon
- 2 tablespoons extra-virgin olive oil
- Salt and pepper to taste
- For the grilled chicken:
- 4 boneless, skinless chicken breasts

- Salt and pepper to taste
- Olive oil (for drizzling)

Instructions:

1. Cauliflower florets should be placed in a food processor and pulsed until they resemble rice grains. Alternatively, you might use a box grater to grind the cauliflower.
2. Combine the riced cauliflower, cherry tomatoes, cucumber, red onion, fresh parsley, fresh mint, extra virgin olive oil, lemon juice, salt, and pepper in a big bowl. Mix thoroughly.
3. Heat your grill or grill pan to a moderately high temperature.
4. Add salt and pepper to the chicken breasts. Add a drizzle of olive oil.
5. Grill the chicken breasts for 6 to 8 minutes on each side or until thoroughly done and the middle is no longer pink. Remove from the heat and give them some time to cool.
6. Cut the chicken breasts from the grill into thin pieces.
7. Place the cooked chicken on top of the cauliflower tabouli and serve.

TURKEY CLUB LETTUCE WRAPS

Ingredients:
- 8 large lettuce leaves (such as iceberg or butter lettuce)
- 1 pound sliced turkey breast
- 8 slices of cooked bacon
- 1 large tomato, thinly sliced
- 1/2 cup mayonnaise
- 1 tablespoon Dijon mustard
- Salt and pepper to taste
- Toothpicks (optional)

Instructions:

1. Spread out and arrange the lettuce leaves on a spotless surface.

2. Fill each lettuce leaf with a few pieces of turkey breast, bacon, and tomato slices.
3. Combine the mayonnaise and Dijon mustard in a small bowl. To taste, add salt and pepper to the food.
4. Drizzle each lettuce wrap's fillings with the mayonnaise mixture.
5. Carefully fold the lettuce leaves and, if desired, secure them with toothpicks.
6. Offer the Turkey Club Lettuce Wraps as a tasty and healthier replacement for regular club sandwiches.

MEDITERRANEAN CHICKPEA SALAD

Ingredients:
- 2 cans (15 ounces each) of chickpeas, rinsed and drained
- 1 cup cherry tomatoes, halved
- 1/2 cup diced cucumber
- 1/2 cup diced red bell pepper
- 1/4 cup sliced Kalamata olives
- 1/4 cup crumbled feta cheese
- 2 tablespoons chopped fresh parsley
- 2 tablespoons chopped fresh mint
- 2 tablespoons extra-virgin olive oil
- 2 tablespoons lemon juice
- 1 clove garlic, minced
- Salt and pepper to taste

Instructions:

1. Place the chickpeas, cherry tomatoes, cucumber, red bell pepper, feta cheese crumbles, sliced Kalamata olives, fresh parsley, and fresh mint in a large bowl.
2. To create the dressing, combine the extra virgin olive oil, lemon juice, minced garlic, salt, and pepper in a small bowl.
3. Drizzle the salad with the dressing, then gently toss to coat all the ingredients.

4. Let the salad sit in the sauce for about 15 minutes to allow the flavors to mingle.
5. Offer the tasty and energizing Mediterranean Chickpea Salad as a light lunch option.

ROASTED VEGGIE QUINOA SALAD

Ingredients:
- 1 cup quinoa
- 2 cups water or vegetable broth
- 1 medium eggplant, diced
- 1 zucchini, diced
- 1 red bell pepper, diced
- 1 yellow bell pepper, diced
- 1 small red onion, sliced
- 2 tablespoons olive oil
- 1 teaspoon dried oregano
- Salt and pepper to taste
- 1/4 cup chopped fresh parsley
- Juice of 1 lemon

Instructions:
1. Set the oven's temperature to 400°F (200°C).
2. Drain the quinoa after giving it a cold water rinse.
3. Bring the water or vegetable broth to a boil in a saucepan. When the quinoa is added, turn the heat down to low, cover the pan, and simmer for 15 to 20 minutes or until the water has been absorbed. Take it off the stove and let it cool.
4. Arrange the diced eggplant, zucchini, red and yellow bell peppers, and red onion on a sizable baking sheet.
5. Drizzle olive oil over the vegetables and season them with salt, pepper, and dried oregano. Toss to coat the vegetables evenly.
6. Cook the vegetables in the oven for 20 to 25 minutes or until they are soft and just beginning to brown. halfway through cooking, stir.

7. In a sizable bowl, combine the cooked quinoa, roasted veggies, fresh parsley that has been chopped, and lemon juice. Toss everything together carefully.
8. If necessary, add more salt and pepper to the dish.
9. Offer the roasted vegetable quinoa salad as a filling or quick lunch

CHICKEN AND AVOCADO CAPRESE SALAD

Ingredients:
- 2 boneless, skinless chicken breasts
- Salt and pepper to taste
- 2 tablespoons olive oil
- 2 cups cherry tomatoes, halved
- 2 cups fresh mozzarella balls (bocconcini), halved
- 1 large avocado, diced
- 1/4 cup chopped fresh basil
- 2 tablespoons balsamic glaze or balsamic vinegar
- Salt and pepper to taste

Instructions:
1. Add salt and pepper to the chicken breasts.
2. In a skillet over medium-high heat, warm the olive oil. Add the chicken breasts and cook for 6 to 8 minutes on each side until the chicken is well cooked and the middle is no longer pink. Remove from the heat and give them some time to cool.
3. Thinly slice the cooked chicken breasts.
4. Combine the cherry tomatoes, fresh mozzarella balls, cubed avocado, and finely chopped fresh basil in a bowl.
5. Add the sliced chicken to the bowl and stir everything together gently.
6. Pour the salad with the balsamic glaze or vinegar.
7. To taste, add salt and pepper to the dish.
8. Serve the Chicken and Avocado Caprese Salad as a robust salad or a filling main meal.

GRILLED STEAK SALAD WITH BLUE CHEESE

Ingredients:
- 1 pound steak (such as sirloin or ribeye)
- Salt and pepper to taste
- 8 cups mixed salad greens
- 1 cup cherry tomatoes, halved
- 1/2 red onion, thinly sliced
- 1/4 cup crumbled blue cheese
- 1/4 cup chopped walnuts (optional)
- Balsamic vinaigrette (for serving)

Instructions:
1. Start your grill or grill pan by heating it to medium-high.
2. Use salt and pepper to season the meat.
3. Grill the steak for 4-6 minutes on each side or until it is cooked to your preference. Take it off the stove and give it some time to cool.
4. Cut the steak from the grill into thin slices.
5. Combine the mixed salad greens, cherry tomatoes, red onion, crumbled blue cheese, and chopped walnuts (if used) in a large bowl.
6. Include the grilled steak slices in the bowl.
7. Dress the salad with the required quantity of balsamic vinaigrette.
8. Gently toss to distribute the ingredients evenly.
9. As a tasty and filling main dish, serve the Grilled Steak Salad with Blue Cheese.

CUCUMBER, TOMATO, AND FETA SALAD

Ingredients:
- 2 large cucumbers, diced
- 2 cups cherry tomatoes, halved
- 1/2 red onion, thinly sliced
- 1/2 cup crumbled feta cheese
- 1/4 cup chopped fresh parsley
- 2 tablespoons extra-virgin olive oil
- 1 tablespoon lemon juice
- Salt and pepper to taste

Instructions:
1. In a big bowl, mix the diced cucumbers, cherry tomatoes, red onion that has been thinly sliced, feta cheese crumbles, and fresh parsley that has been chopped.
2. To make the dressing, combine the extra virgin olive oil, lemon juice, salt, and pepper in a small bowl.
3. After adding the sauce to the salad, gently toss the ingredients in the dressing to combine.
4. Let the salad sit for 10-15 minutes to allow the flavors to mingle.
5. Offer the cucumber, tomato, and feta salad as a light lunch or a vivid, energizing side dish.

ASIAN CHICKEN SALAD WITH PEANUT DRESSING

Ingredients: For the salad:
- 4 cups mixed salad greens
- 2 cups cooked chicken breast, shredded or diced
- 1 cup shredded carrots
- 1 cup thinly sliced cabbage
- 1/2 cup chopped red bell pepper
- 1/2 cup chopped cucumber
- 1/4 cup chopped green onions
- 1/4 cup chopped cilantro
- 1/4 cup chopped peanuts (optional, for garnish)

For the peanut dressing:

- 1/4 cup creamy peanut butter
- 2 tablespoons soy sauce
- 2 tablespoons rice vinegar
- 1 tablespoon honey or maple syrup
- 1 tablespoon sesame oil
- 1 clove garlic, minced
- 1/2 teaspoon grated fresh ginger
- Water (as needed to thin the dressing)
- Salt and pepper to taste

Instructions:

1. Combine the mixed salad greens, cooked chicken breast, shredded carrots, cabbage slices, diced red bell pepper, cucumber, chopped green onions, and cilantro in a large salad bowl.
2. To create the dressing, combine the sesame oil, peanut butter, soy sauce, rice vinegar, honey or maple syrup, chopped garlic, grated ginger, salt, and pepper in a separate small bowl.
3. Add a tablespoon of water to the dressing until the desired consistency is achieved. The sauce ought to be thick yet pourable.

4. After adding the peanut dressing, gently toss the salad to distribute the sauce evenly.
5. As a garnish, top with chopped peanuts, if using.
6. Offer the tasty and filling Asian Chicken Salad with Peanut Dressing as a main course.

CHICKEN AND VEGGIE KABOBS

Ingredients:
- 2 boneless, skinless chicken breasts cut into chunks
- 1 bell pepper, cut into chunks
- 1 zucchini, sliced into rounds
- 1 red onion, cut into chunks
- Cherry tomatoes
- 2 tablespoons olive oil
- 2 tablespoons soy sauce
- 1 tablespoon honey or maple syrup
- 1 teaspoon garlic powder
- 1/2 teaspoon ground cumin
- 1/2 teaspoon paprika
- Salt and pepper to taste
- Skewers (if using wooden skewers, soak them in water for about 30 minutes before grilling)

Instructions:
1. Combine the olive oil, soy sauce, honey or maple syrup, garlic powder, ground cumin, paprika, salt, and pepper to make the marinade.
2. Include the marinade with the chicken chunks and toss to coat. Refrigerate the chicken for at least 30 minutes or overnight while it marinates.
3. Heat your grill or grill pan to a moderately high temperature.
4. Alternately thread cherry tomatoes, bell pepper, zucchini, red onion, and marinated chicken parts onto skewers.

5. Grill the chicken and vegetable kabobs for 10 to 12 minutes, turning them over halfway through or until the chicken is cooked and the vegetables are soft.
6. Take them off the grill and give them some time to cool.
7. Present the Chicken and Veggie Kabobs as a tasty and eye-catching main dish.

SPICY TURKEY AND CAULIFLOWER RICE BOWL

Ingredients:
- 1 pound ground turkey
- 2 cups cauliflower rice
- 1 bell pepper, diced
- 1 small onion, diced
- 2 cloves garlic, minced
- 1 tablespoon olive oil
- 1 tablespoon soy sauce or tamari
- 1 teaspoon ground cumin
- 1/2 teaspoon chili powder
- 1/4 teaspoon cayenne pepper (adjust to taste)
- Salt and pepper to taste
- Fresh cilantro (for garnish)

Instructions:
1. Place a large skillet over medium heat and add the olive oil.
2. Add the minced garlic and onion to the skillet and cook until the garlic is fragrant and the onion is transparent.
3. When the ground turkey is brown and done, add it to the skillet and heat it, breaking it up with a spoon.
4. Add the cauliflower rice, diced bell pepper, soy sauce or tamari, cumin powder, chili powder, cayenne pepper, salt, and pepper. Cook the cauliflower rice for 5-7 minutes or until it has heated through.

5. Taste-test the seasoning and, if necessary, add additional salt, pepper, or spices.
6. Take it off the fire and give it some time to cool.
7. Garnish Spicy Turkey and Cauliflower Rice Bowl with fresh cilantro and serve it hot.

GRILLED LEMON HERB TUNA STEAKS

Ingredients:
- 2 tuna steaks
- Juice of 1 lemon
- 2 tablespoons olive oil
- 2 cloves garlic, minced
- 1 tablespoon chopped fresh herbs (such as parsley, basil, or thyme)
- Salt and pepper to taste
- Lemon wedges (for serving)

Instructions:
1. Start your grill or grill pan by heating it to medium-high.
2. To make the marinade, combine the lemon juice, olive oil, minced garlic, finely chopped fresh herbs, salt, and pepper in a bowl.
3. Spoon the marinade over the tuna steaks placed in a shallow dish. For 15 to 30 minutes, let them marinate.
4. Grill the tuna steaks on each side for two to three minutes until they reach the desired doneness.
5. Take them off the grill and give them some time to cool.
6. Put lemon wedges on the side and plate the grilled lemon herb tuna steaks.

CHICKEN AND BLACK BEAN-STUFFED PEPPERS

Ingredients:
- 4 bell peppers (any color)
- 1 pound ground chicken
- 1 cup cooked black beans
- 1/2 cup diced onion
- 1/2 cup chopped bell pepper
- 2 cloves garlic, minced
- 1 teaspoon ground cumin
- 1 teaspoon chili powder
- 1/2 teaspoon paprika
- Salt and pepper to taste
- Shredded cheese (such as cheddar or Monterey Jack) for topping
- Fresh cilantro (for garnish)

Instructions:
1. Set the oven's temperature to 375°F (190°C).
2. Cut off the bell peppers' tops, then scoop out the seeds and membranes.
3. Brown the ground chicken in a sizable skillet over medium heat. Remove any extra fat.
4. Fill the skillet with the diced onion, bell pepper, minced garlic, chili powder, paprika, salt, and pepper. Sauté the vegetables until they are soft.
5. Add the cooked black beans and heat through for a few more minutes.
6. Fill each bell pepper to the brim with the chicken-and-black-bean mixture.
7. Put the peppers in a baking tray after being filled. Each pepper should have cheese shredded on top of it.
8. Bake in the preheated oven for 25 to 30 minutes or until the cheese is melted and bubbling and the peppers are soft.
9. Take them out of the oven and cool a bit before serving.

10. If preferred, garnish with fresh cilantro.
11. The stuffed peppers with chicken and black beans are a tasty and filling main dish.

KETO EGG ROLL IN A BOWL

Ingredients:
- 1 pound ground pork or ground turkey
- 1 small onion, thinly sliced
- 1 small carrot, shredded
- 4 cups shredded cabbage or coleslaw mix
- 3 cloves garlic, minced
- 2 tablespoons soy sauce or tamari
- 1 tablespoon sesame oil
- 1/2 teaspoon ground ginger
- Salt and pepper to taste
- Green onions (for garnish)

Instructions:
1. Brown and fry the ground pork or turkey over medium-high heat in a sizable skillet or wok. Remove any extra fat.
2. Move the cooked meat to one side of the skillet and add the shredded carrot and onion to the other. Sauté until the carrot begins to soften and the onion turns transparent.
3. Fill the skillet with the minced garlic, shredded cabbage or coleslaw mix, sesame oil, soy sauce or tamari, ground ginger, salt, and pepper. To combine everything, stir.
4. Continue to boil the cabbage, stirring often, until it wilts and reaches the desired softness.
5. Taste-test the dish and add more salt or soy sauce as desired.
6. Take it off the fire and give it some time to cool.
7. Add sliced green onions as a garnish.
8. Offer the delicious low-carb Keto Egg Roll in a Bowl instead of regular egg rolls.

CAULIFLOWER HUMMUS WITH VEGGIE STICKS

Ingredients:

- 1 small head of cauliflower, cut into florets
- 3 tablespoons tahini
- 3 tablespoons lemon juice
- 2 cloves garlic, minced
- 2 tablespoons olive oil
- 1/2 teaspoon ground cumin
- Salt and pepper to taste
- Assorted veggies for dipping (carrot sticks, cucumber slices, bell pepper strips, etc.)

Instructions:

1. To make the cauliflower florets soft, steam them.
2. Combine the steamed cauliflower, tahini, lemon juice, minced garlic, extra virgin olive oil, ground cumin, salt, and pepper in a food processor.
3. Process the mixture until it is creamy and smooth, stopping to scrape the sides as necessary.
4. Taste and, if necessary, adjust the seasoning.
5. Place the hummus made from cauliflower in a serving bowl.
6. Offer vegetable sticks for dipping alongside the cauliflower hummus.
7. Use the cauliflower hummus and veggie sticks as a tasty and nutritious snack or starter.

TOFU SCRAMBLE BREAKFAST BURRITO

Ingredients:
- 1 block (14-16 ounces) firm tofu, drained and crumbled
- 1 tablespoon olive oil
- 1/2 small onion, diced
- 1 bell pepper, diced
- 2 cloves garlic, minced
- 1 teaspoon ground cumin
- 1/2 teaspoon ground turmeric
- Salt and pepper to taste
- 4 large tortillas
- Salsa, avocado slices, and chopped cilantro (optional, for serving)

Instructions:
1. In a skillet over medium heat, warm the olive oil.
2. Add the bell pepper and onion dice to the skillet and cook until the vegetables are tender.
3. Fill the skillet with the minced garlic, crumbled tofu, ground cumin, turmeric, salt, and pepper.
4. Heat the tofu and lightly brown it for 5-7 minutes while stirring occasionally.
5. Use a different skillet or a microwave to reheat the tortillas.
6. Distribute the tofu scrambillas, distributing it evenly throughout each one.
7. Add salsa, avocado slices, and chopped cilantro to the tofu scramble as desired.
8. To make burritos, foldtightlyhe tortillas' sidd roll them up tightly.
9. Warm the breakfast burritos with tofu scramble.
10. Enjoy as a filling and tasty option for breakfast or brunch.

CHAPTER 4:
RECIPE FOR DINNER

GRILLED CHICKEN AND AVOCADO SALSA

Ingredients: For the grilled chicken:
- 2 boneless, skinless chicken breasts
- 2 tablespoons olive oil
- 1 teaspoon ground cumin
- 1 teaspoon chili powder
- Salt and pepper to taste

For the avocado salsa:

- 1 ripe avocado, diced
- 1 small tomato, diced
- 1/4 cup diced red onion
- 2 tablespoons chopped fresh cilantro
- Juice of 1 lime
- Salt and pepper to taste

Instructions:

1. Start your grill or grill pan by heati
2. Combine a small bowl, combine the olive oil, ground cumin, chili po in a small bowlwder, salt, and pepper.
3. Evenly coat the chicken breasts with the spice mixture by brushing it on.
4. Grilon each side l the chicken breasnutes on each side or until the inside is fully cooked and no longer pink. Remove from the heat and give th
5. Placee avocado salsa, place the diced avocado, tomato, red onion, cilantro, lime juice, salt, and pep to make the avocado salsaper in a separate bowl. Gently blend by tossing.

6. Cut the cooked chicken breasts into slices and serve them with the salsa made from avocados.
7. Savor the grilled chicken and avocado salsa as a tasty and nutritious main dish.

BEEF AND BROCCOLI STIR-FRY

Ingredients:
- 1 pound beef sirloin or flank steak, thinly sliced
- 3 tablespoons soy sauce
- 2 tablespoons oyster sauce
- 2 tablespoons hoisin sauce
- 1 tablespoon cornstarch
- 2 tablespoons vegetable oil
- 3 cloves garlic, minced
- 1 teaspoon grated fresh ginger
- 4 cups broccoli florets
- Salt and pepper to taste
- Cooked rice or noodles

Instructions:
1. Combineake the sauce, combine the cornstarch, soy sauce, oyster sauce, and
2. to make the saucehoisin sauce inHeate skillet or wok, heat the vegeta in a sizable skillet or wokblAddt.
3. To the skillet, add minced garlic to the skillet and the grated ginger, and cook for approximately a minute or until fragrant.
4. Stir-fry the beef that has been thinly sliced in the skillet for 2–3 minutes or until it is browned.
5. When the broccoli is tender-crisp, add the broccoli florets to the skifry for 3–4 minutes.
6. Cover the beef and broccoli in the skillet with the sauce. Stir to distribute the coating evenly.

7. Continue to cookfurther minute or two or until the sauce is thick.
8. To taste, add salt and pepper to the dish.
9. Take it off the fire and give it some time to cool.
10. Put the cook or noodles on top of the beef and broccoli stir-fry.
11. Devour as a tasty and filling stir-fry dish.

ZUCCHINI NOODLES WITH PESTO AND GRILLED CHICKEN

Ingredients: For the zucchini noodles:
- 4 medium zucchini
- 1 tablespoon olive oil
- Salt and pepper to taste

For the pesto:

- 2 cups fresh basil leaves
- 1/4 cup pine nuts (or substitute with walnuts or almonds)
- 2 cloves garlic
- 1/4 cup grated Parmesan cheese
- Juice of 1 lemon
- 1/4 cup olive oil
- Salt and pepper to taste

For the grilled chicken:

- 2 boneless, skinless chicken breasts
- Salt and pepper to taste
- Olive oil (for grilling)

Instructions:

1. To make zucchini noodles, use a julienne peeler or a spiralizer.

2. In a big skillet over medium heat, warm the olive oil. Zucchini noodles should be added and cooked for two to three minutes until crisp and tender. Add salt and pepper to taste. Heat has bee
3. Mix a food processor, mix the basil leaves, pine nuts, garlic, shredded Parmesan cheese, lemon juice, extra virgin olivr in a food processoe oil, salt, and pepper. Pulse the ingredients until they are well combined and smooth. If necessary, adjust the seasoning.
4. Heat your grill or grill pan to a high temperature.
5. Add salt and pepper to the chicken breasts. Add a drizzle of olive oil.
6. Grilon each side l the chicken breasnutes on each side or until the insides are entirely done and no longer pink. Remove from the heat and give them some time to cool. The grilled chicken should be cut into tiny strips.
7. Combine the pesto sauce and zucchini noodles in a large bowl and toss to combine.
8. Arrange the grilled chicken slices on top of the zucchini noodles on each serving platter.
9. The grilled chicken and zucchini noodles with pesto are a tasty and nutritious main dish.

LEMON-GARLIC SHRIMP AND ASPARAGUS

Ingredients:
- 1 pound large shrimp, peeled and deveined
- 1 bunch, asparagus, trimmed
- 2 tablespoons olive oil
- 4 cloves garlic, minced
- Juice of 1 lemon
- Zest of 1 lemon
- Salt and pepper to taste

Instructions:

1. Start your grill or grill pan by heating it to medium-high.

2. Mix the shrimp, asparagus, lemon juice, lemon zest, chopped garlic, salt, and pepper in a bowl. Toss to coat everything evenly.
3. Skewer the asparagus and shrimp together.
4. Grill the asparagus and shrimp skewers on each side for 2 to 3 minutes or until the asparagus is crisp-tender and the shrimp are opaque.
5. Take them off the grill and give them some time to cool.
6. Present the shrimp with asparagus and lemon-garlic sauce as a tasty and healthy main dish.

SEARED AHI TUNA SALAD

Ingredients:
- 2 ahi tuna steaks
- Salt and pepper to taste
- 2 tablespoons sesame seeds
- 4 cups mixed salad greens
- 1 cucumber, thinly sliced
- 1 carrot, shredded
- 1/2 red onion, thinly sliced
- 1 avocado, sliced
- 2 tablespoons soy sauce or tamari
- 1 tablespoon rice vinegar
- 1 tablespoon sesame oil
- 1 teaspoon honey or maple syrup (optional)

Instructions:
1. Add salt and pepper to the ahi tuna steaks.
2. On a dish, spread the sesame seeds out, then press the tuna steaks into them to completely cover them.
3. Put a grill pan or skillet on high heat. Pour a little oil into the pan.
4. Grill the tuna steaks for 1-2 minutes per side or until the outsides are charred but the centers are still pink. Remove from the heat and give them some time to cool. The seared tuna should be cut into tiny slices.

5. Combine the mixed salad greens, sliced cucumber, shredded carrot, thinly sliced red onion, and sliced avocado in a sizable salad bowl.
6. To create the dressing, combine the soy sauce or tamari, rice vinegar, sesame oil, honey or maple syrup (if using), and sesame seeds in a small dish.
7. Pour the salad dressing over it and gently mix the items to coat them all.
8. Arrange the seared ahi tuna slices on top of the salad.
9. Present the Seared Ahi Tuna Salad as a tasty and enticing main dish.

TURKEY ZUCCHINI MEATBALLS

Ingredients:
- 1 pound ground turkey
- 1 zucchini, grated and excess moisture squeezed out
- 1/4 cup breadcrumbs (gluten-free if desired)
- 1/4 cup grated Parmesan cheese
- 2 cloves garlic, minced
- 2 tablespoons chopped fresh parsley
- 1 teaspoon dried oregano
- 1/2 teaspoon salt
- 1/4 teaspoon black pepper
- Olive oil (for cooking)
- Marinara sauce (for serving)

Instructions:
1. Ground turkey, grated zucchini, breadcrumbs, grated Parmesan cheese, minced garlic, chopped fresh parsley, dried oregano, salt, and black pepper should all be combined in a big bowl. Blend thoroughly.
2. Create meatballs of the desired size using the ingredients.
3. Warm a thin layer of olive oil in a skillet set over medium heat.
4. After adding the meatballs to the skillet, heat them for 8 to 10 minutes or until they are cooked through and

browned. To ensure even browning, turn them occasionally.
5. Take them out of the skillet and give them some time to cool.
6. Offer the turkey zucchini meatballs with spaghetti, rice, salad, and marinara sauce for dipping.

CREAMY TUSCAN CHICKEN SKILLET

Ingredients:
- 4 boneless, skinless chicken breasts
- Salt and pepper to taste
- 2 tablespoons olive oil
- 4 cloves garlic, minced
- 1 cup cherry tomatoes, halved
- 1 cup baby spinach leaves
- 1/2 cup sun-dried tomatoes, chopped
- 1 cup heavy cream
- 1/4 cup grated Parmesan cheese
- Fresh basil leaves (for garnish)

Instructions:
1. Add salt and pepper to the chicken breasts.
2. In a skillet over medium heat, warm the olive oil. Add the chicken breasts and cook for 6 to 8 minutes on each side until the chicken is well cooked and the middle is no longer pink. Remove from the heat and give them some time to cool. The cooked chicken should be cut into thin strips.
3. Add the minced garlic to the same skillet and sauté until fragrant.
4. Include the sun-dried tomatoes, sun-dried cherry tomatoes, and baby spinach leaves in the skillet. Sauté the cherry tomatoes and spinach until the spinach has wilted.
5. Add the grated Parmesan cheese and heavy cream. Simmer the mixture after giving it one more stir. The

sauce needs to be cooked for a few minutes until it thickens.
6. Add the sliced cooked chicken to the skillet and combine the ingredients.
7. Take it off the fire and give it some time to cool.
8. Top the hot, Creamy Tuscan Chicken Skillet with fresh basil leaves before serving.

BLACKENED SALMON WITH AVOCADO SALSA

Ingredients:

For the blackened salmon:

- 4 salmon fillets
- 1 tablespoon paprika
- 1 teaspoon garlic powder
- 1 teaspoon onion powder
- 1 teaspoon dried thyme
- 1 teaspoon dried oregano
- 1/2 teaspoon cayenne pepper (adjust to taste)
- Salt and pepper to taste
- 2 tablespoons olive oil

For the avocado salsa:

- 1 avocado, diced
- 1/2 cup diced tomatoes
- 1/4 cup diced red onion
- Juice of 1 lime
- 2 tablespoons chopped fresh cilantro
- Salt and pepper to taste

Instructions:

1. Start your grill or grill pan by heating it to medium-high.
2. To make the blackened seasoning, combine the paprika, garlic powder, onion powder, dried thyme, oregano, cayenne pepper, salt, and pepper.

3. Rub the blackened seasoning onto both sides of the fish fillets after brushing them with olive oil.
4. Grill the salmon fillets on each side for 4 to 5 minutes until they are cooked through and fall apart easily when tested with a fork. Remove from the heat and give them some time to cool.
5. Place diced avocado, tomatoes, red onion, lime juice, finely chopped fresh cilantro, salt, and pepper in a separate bowl to make the avocado salsa. Gently blend by tossing.
6. Spoon the avocado salsa on top of the blackened salmon fillets before serving.
7. Savor the blackened salmon with avocado salsa as a savory and healthy main dish.

CHICKEN FAJITA STUFFED PEPPERS

Ingredients:
- 4 bell peppers (any color)
- 2 chicken breasts, thinly sliced
- 1 tablespoon olive oil
- 1 onion, thinly sliced
- 1 red bell pepper, thinly sliced
- 1 green bell pepper, thinly sliced
- 2 cloves garlic, minced
- 1 tablespoon chili powder
- 1 teaspoon ground cumin
- 1/2 teaspoon paprika
- Salt and pepper to taste
- Shredded cheese (such as cheddar or Monterey Jack)
- Fresh cilantro (for garnish)

Instructions:
1. Set the oven's temperature to 375°F (190°C).
2. Cut off the bell peppers' tops, then scoop out the seeds and membranes.

3. In a skillet over medium-high heat, warm the olive oil. Slices of chicken should not be pink when they are added and cooked. Take out of the skillet, then set it aside.
4. Include the green bell pepper, red bell pepper, and onion slices in the same skillet. When they are soft, sauté.
5. Season the skillet with salt, pepper, paprika, chili powder, ground cumin, and chopped garlic. Cook for another minute while stirring.
6. Add the vegetables and seasonings to the skillet along with the cooked chicken.
7. Stuff the chicken fajita mixture into each bell pepper.
8. Put the peppers in a baking tray after being filled. Each pepper should have cheese shredded on top of it.
9. Bake for 25 to 30 minutes in a preheated oven or until the cheese is melted and bubbling and the peppers are soft.
10. Take them out of the oven and give them a brief cooling period before serving.
11. If preferred, garnish with fresh cilantro.
12. Offer the Chicken Fajita Stuffed Peppers as an enticing and filling main meal.

GARLIC BUTTER BAKED COD

Ingredients:
- 4 cod fillets
- 4 tablespoons unsalted butter, melted
- 4 cloves garlic, minced
- 2 tablespoons lemon juice
- 1 teaspoon dried parsley
- Salt and pepper to taste
- Lemon wedges (for serving)
- Fresh parsley (for garnish)

Instructions:
1. Set the oven's temperature to 375°F (190°C).
2. Cod fillets should be placed in a baking dish.

3. Mix the melted butter, minced garlic, lemon juice, dried parsley, salt, and pepper in a small bowl. To blend, thoroughly stir.
4. Cover the cod fillets equally with the garlic butter mixture.
5. Bake the fish in the oven for 12 to 15 minutes or until it is opaque and flakes readily.
6. Take them out of the oven and give them some time to cool.
7. Put lemon wedges on the side and serve the baked cod with garlic butter.
8. If preferred, garnish with fresh parsley.

KETO CHILI WITH CAULIFLOWER RICE

Ingredients: For the chili:
- 1 pound ground beef
- 1 onion, diced
- 2 cloves garlic, minced
- 1 bell pepper, diced
- 1 can diced tomatoes
- 1 can tomato sauce
- 2 tablespoons chili powder
- 1 teaspoon ground cumin
- 1 teaspoon paprika
- 1/2 teaspoon dried oregano
- 1/4 teaspoon cayenne pepper (adjust to taste)
- Salt and pepper to taste
- Olive oil (for cooking)

For the cauliflower rice:

- 1 small head of cauliflower, riced
- 2 tablespoons olive oil
- Salt and pepper to taste

Instructions:

1. Heat the olive oil over medium heat in a big pot or Dutch oven. Add the diced bell pepper, minced garlic, and diced onion. Sauté the vegetables until they are tender.
2. Add the ground beef to the pot and boil it until it is browned. Remove any extra fat.
3. Add the diced tomatoes, tomato sauce, cayenne pepper, paprika, dried oregano, chili powder, ground cumin, salt, and pepper. Mix thoroughly.
4. Lower the heat to a low setting and simmer the chili for about 30 minutes to let the flavors blend. If necessary, adjust the seasoning.
5. In the meantime, heat the olive oil in a separate skillet over medium heat. Cook the riced cauliflower until it is soft after being added. To taste, add salt and pepper to the food.
6. Include a side of cauliflower rice with the keto chili. Enjoy!

SPINACH AND FETA STUFFED PORK CHOPS

Ingredients:
- 4 boneless pork chops
- 2 cups fresh spinach leaves
- 1/2 cup crumbled feta cheese
- 2 cloves garlic, minced
- 1 tablespoon olive oil
- Salt and pepper to taste

Instructions:
1. Set the oven's temperature to 375°F (190°C).
2. Cut a pocket for the stuffing into each pork chop. Take care just to cut partially through.
3. Warm up the olive oil in a skillet over medium heat. Sauté the minced garlic until fragrant after adding it.
4. Stir in the fresh spinach leaves and heat them in the skillet until they wilt. Get rid of the heat.

5. Add feta cheese and a portion of the sautéed spinach to each pork chop.
6. Sprinkle salt and pepper on the filled pork chops.
7. Bring a different skillet to medium-high heat. The stuffed pork chops should be added and seared until browned on both sides.
8. Place the seared pork chops in a baking dish and bake in the oven for 20 to 25 minutes or until the internal temperature reaches 145 degrees Fahrenheit (63 degrees Celsius).
9. Take them out of the oven and give them time to cool before serving.
10. As a tasty main dish, offer spinach and feta-stuffed pork chops.

ROSEMARY DIJON LAMB CHOPS

Ingredients:
- 4 lamb chops
- 2 tablespoons Dijon mustard
- 2 tablespoons fresh rosemary, chopped
- 2 cloves garlic, minced
- 2 tablespoons olive oil
- Salt and pepper to taste

Instructions:
1. Start your grill or grill pan by heating it to medium-high.
2. To make the marinade, combine the Dijon mustard, minced garlic, fresh rosemary that has been diced, olive oil, salt, and pepper in a small bowl.
3. Brush the marinade over the lamb chops, covering all sides.
4. Grill the lamb chops for 3 to 4 minutes on each side or until they are cooked to your preference.
5. Take them off the grill and give them some time to rest before serving.

6. Offer delicious and tender Rosemary Dijon Lamb Chops as a main course.

TURKEY MEATLOAF WITH ROASTED VEGETABLES

Ingredients: For the meatloaf:
- 1 ½ pounds of ground turkey
- 1 small onion, finely chopped
- 2 cloves garlic, minced
- 1 carrot, grated
- 1/4 cup breadcrumbs (gluten-free if desired)
- 1/4 cup ketchup
- 1 tablespoon Worcestershire sauce
- 1 tablespoon Dijon mustard
- 1 tablespoon chopped fresh parsley
- 1 teaspoon dried thyme
- 1 teaspoon dried oregano
- Salt and pepper to taste

For the roasted vegetables:

- Assorted vegetables (such as potatoes, carrots, and Brussels sprouts), cut into chunks
- 2 tablespoons olive oil
- Salt and pepper to taste

Instructions:
1. Set the oven's temperature to 375°F (190°C).
2. Combine the breadcrumbs, ketchup, Worcestershire sauce, Dijon mustard, chopped fresh parsley, dried thyme, dried oregano, finely diced onion, minced garlic, shredded carrot, salt, and pepper in a big bowl. Blend thoroughly.
3. Form the turkey mixture into a loaf and put it in a baking dish that has been buttered.
4. Combine the chopped veggies with olive oil, salt, and pepper in another bowl.

5. In the baking dish, place the vegetables around the turkey meatloaf.
6. Bake for 45 to 50 minutes in a preheated oven or until the meatloaf is done and the vegetables are soft.
7. Take it out of the range and allow it to cool before slicing.
8. Make the turkey meatloaf with roasted vegetables into a hearty main dish for a pleasant meal.

SHRIMP AND CAULIFLOWER GRITS

Ingredients: For the shrimp:
- 1 pound shrimp, peeled and deveined
- 2 tablespoons olive oil
- 3 cloves garlic, minced
- 1 teaspoon paprika
- Salt and pepper to taste
- Fresh parsley (for garnish)

For the cauliflower grits:

- 1 large head of cauliflower, cut into florets
- 2 tablespoons butter
- 1/4 cup grated Parmesan cheese
- Salt and pepper to taste

Instructions:

1. Heat the olive oil in a big skillet over medium heat. Sauté the minced garlic until fragrant after adding it.
2. Place the shrimp in the skillet and cook for two to three minutes on each side or until they are cooked and pink. Add paprika, salt, and pepper for seasoning. Heat has been removed; set aside.
3. Till the cauliflower florets are soft, steam or boil them.
4. Add the cooked cauliflower to a food processor and pulse it until it resembles rice.

5. Melt the butter in a separate skillet over medium heat. Add the riced cauliflower and heat through for a few minutes.
6. Add the Parmesan cheese that has been grated, then season with salt and pepper to taste.
7. Arrange the cooked shrimp on top of the cauliflower grits.
8. Add fresh parsley as a garnish.
9. Enjoy the tasty and low-carb Shrimp and Cauliflower Grits as a main dish.

EGGPLANT ROLLATINI

Ingredients:
- 2 large eggplants, sliced lengthwise into 1/4-inch thick slices
- 2 cups ricotta cheese
- 1/2 cup grated Parmesan cheese
- 1/4 cup chopped fresh basil
- 2 cloves garlic, minced
- 2 cups marinara sauce
- 1 1/2 cups shredded mozzarella cheese
- Salt and pepper to taste
- Olive oil (for cooking)

Instructions:
1. Set the oven's temperature to 375°F (190°C).
2. To release extra moisture, lightly salt the eggplant slices and allow them to sit for 10 minutes. Use a paper towel to dry.
3. Bring olive oil to a simmer in a skillet. Slices of eggplant should be added and cooked for two to three minutes on each side or until tender and gently browned. Heat has been removed; set aside.
4. Mix the ricotta cheese with the grated Parmesan cheese, fresh basil that has been chopped, minced garlic, salt, and pepper in a bowl. Mix thoroughly.

5. Cover the bottom of a baking dish with a thin coating of marinara sauce.
6. Spoon the ricotta mixture onto one end of an eggplant slice. The eggplant slice should be rolled up and placed seam-side down in the baking pan.
7. Repeat with the rest of the ricotta mixture and eggplant pieces.
8. Cover the rolled eggplant slices with the leftover marinara sauce in the baking dish.
9. Top with some shredded mozzarella cheese.
10. Bake in the oven for 20 to 25 minutes, or until the cheese is melted and bubbling
11. Please remove it from the range and set it aside to cool before serving.
12. Offer the vegetarian main course, the Eggplant Rollatini, as a tasty and delectable dish.

CHICKEN AND MUSHROOM SKILLET WITH CREAM SAUCE

Ingredients:
- 4 boneless, skinless chicken breasts
- Salt and pepper to taste
- 2 tablespoons olive oil
- 8 ounces mushrooms, sliced
- 3 cloves garlic, minced
- 1 cup chicken broth
- 1 cup heavy cream
- 1 teaspoon dried thyme
- 1 tablespoon chopped fresh parsley (for garnish)

Instructions:
1. Add salt and pepper to the chicken breasts.
2. In a big skillet over medium heat, warm the olive oil. Add the chicken breasts and cook for 6 to 8 minutes on each side until the chicken is well cooked and the middle is no longer pink. Take out of the skillet, then set it aside.
3. Place the sliced mushrooms and minced garlic in the same skillet. Sauté the garlic and mushrooms until the former are aromatic.
4. Add the chicken broth after scraping any browned bits from the skillet's bottom.
5. Fill the skillet with the heavy cream and dried thyme. To blend, thoroughly stir.
6. Simmer the ingredients for a few minutes to let the sauce thicken gradually
7. After cooking, add the chicken breasts back to the skillet, and let them heat through for a few minutes.
8. Take it off the fire and give it some time to cool.
9. Add freshly cut parsley as a garnish.
10. As a hearty and savory main dish, serve the Cream Sauced Chicken and Mushroom Skillet.

ITALIAN SAUSAGE AND KALE SOUP

Ingredients:
- 1 pound Italian sausage, casings removed
- 1 onion, diced
- 3 cloves garlic, minced
- 4 cups chicken broth
- 1 can diced tomatoes
- 1 bunch, kale, stems removed and leaves chopped
- 1 teaspoon dried oregano
- 1 teaspoon dried basil
- Salt and pepper to taste
- Grated Parmesan cheese (for serving)

Instructions:
1. Brown and sauté the Italian sausage in a large pot or Dutch oven over medium heat. Use a wooden spoon to cut it into smaller pieces.
2. Add the onion dice to the pot and cook until transparent.
3. Stir in the minced garlic, cooking for an additional minute until aromatic.
4. Add the diced tomatoes with juices and the chicken broth. To blend, thoroughly stir.
5. Bring the soup to a simmer and cook it for about 15 minutes to enable the flavors to mingle.
6. Fill the saucepan with the chopped kale, salt, pepper, dried oregano, and dried basil. Kale should be wilted and soft after 5 to 10 minutes of stirring and cooking.
7. Taste and, if necessary, adjust the seasoning.
8. Place grated Parmesan cheese on top of the Italian sausage and kale soup in bowls.
9. If wanted, serve the soup hot with crusty bread.

BAKED CHICKEN AND VEGETABLE FOIL PACKETS

Ingredients:
- 4 boneless, skinless chicken breasts
- 2 cups mixed vegetables (such as bell peppers, zucchini, and carrots), sliced
- 1/4 cup olive oil
- 2 cloves garlic, minced
- 1 teaspoon dried Italian seasoning
- Salt and pepper to taste
- Lemon slices (for garnish)
- Fresh parsley (for garnish)

Instructions:
1. Set the oven's temperature to 425°F (220°C).
2. Make four aluminum foil sheets that are big enough to wrap each chicken breast and each vegetable.
3. In the middle of each foil sheet, place a chicken breast.
4. Combine the sliced mixed veggies, salt, pepper, olive oil, chopped garlic, and dried Italian seasoning in a bowl. Toss to distribute the seasoning combination over the vegetables evenly.
5. Distribute the vegetable mixture among the foil pouches, enclosing the chicken breasts.
6. To make a packet with the chicken and vegetables inside, fold the foil securely and seal it.
7. Put the foil-wrapped packages on a baking sheet and bake for 25 to 30 minutes until the chicken is cooked and the vegetables are soft.
8. Open the foil packets with caution, being mindful of the steam. Place the veggies and chicken on serving dishes.
9. Add lemon slices and fresh parsley as garnish.
10. As a tasty and simple-to-prepare main course, serve the Baked Chicken and Vegetable Foil Packets.

SPAGHETTI SQUASH CARBONARA

Ingredients:
- 1 medium spaghetti squash
- 6 slices bacon, chopped
- 2 cloves garlic, minced
- 2 large eggs
- 1/2 cup grated Parmesan cheese
- Salt and pepper to taste
- Fresh parsley (for garnish)

Instructions:
1. Set the oven's temperature to 400°F (200°C).
2. Remove the seeds from the spaghetti squash by cutting it in half lengthwise.
3. Position the spaghetti squash halves on a baking sheet with the sliced side up.
4. Bake in the oven for 40 to 50 minutes or until the flesh is soft and readily shredded into spaghetti-like strands with a fork. Allow it to cool a little.
5. Over medium heat, sauté the diced bacon until crisp while the spaghetti squash bakes. The bacon drippings should stay in the skillet when you remove them and set them aside.
6. Add the minced garlic and cook in the same skillet for one minute or until fragrant.
7. Combine the eggs and grated Parmesan cheese in a bowl. Place aside.
8. To make spaghetti squash strands, use a fork to scrape the cooked spaghetti squash's flesh.
9. Include the spaghetti squash strands with the bacon and garlic drippings in the skillet. Toss the strands to distribute the drippings evenly.
10. Turn off the heat under the skillet and rapidly whisk the egg and cheese mixture with the spaghetti squash to evenly coat the strands. The skillet's heat will cook the eggs.

11. Add pepper and salt to taste.
12. Place the skillet back over low heat, and cook for one more minute while gently stirring or until the sauce thickens gradually.
13. Top with the crispy bacon.
14. Add fresh parsley as a garnish.
15. Serving spaghetti squash carbonara as a lighter and healthier alternative to regular pasta carbonara.

GRILLED FLANK STEAK WITH CHIMICHURRI SAUCE

Ingredients: For the flank steak:
- 1 ½ pounds flank steak
- Salt and pepper to taste
- Olive oil (for brushing)

For the chimichurri sauce:

- 1 cup fresh parsley leaves, packed
- 1/4 cup fresh cilantro leaves, packed
- 3 cloves garlic
- 2 tablespoons red wine vinegar
- 1/2 teaspoon red pepper flakes
- 1/2 teaspoon dried oregano
- 1/2 cup olive oil
- Salt and pepper to taste

Instructions:
1. Set the grill to a medium-high temperature.
2. Season the flank steak on both sides with salt and pepper.
3. To keep the steak from adhering to the grill, lightly brush it with olive oil.
4. Grill the flank steak for 4-6 minutes on each side or until it is cooked to your preference.
5. Take the steak off the grill and give it some time to rest.

6. Make the chimichurri sauce while the meat is resting. Combine the parsley, cilantro, garlic, red wine vinegar, red pepper flakes, and dried oregano in a food processor or blender. To finely chop the items, continue to pulse.
7. Add the olive oil in a steady stream while the food processor or blender runs until the sauce is smooth. To taste, add salt and pepper to the food.
8. Cut the cooked flank steak into thin strips against the grain.
9. Drizzle copious amounts of chimichurri sauce over the cooked flank steak before serving.
10. Savor the grilled flank steak with chimichurri sauce as a tasty and filling main dish.

PESTO CHICKEN-STUFFED PORTOBELLO MUSHROOMS

Ingredients:
- 4 large portobello mushrooms
- 2 boneless, skinless chicken breasts
- 1/4 cup basil pesto
- 1/2 cup shredded mozzarella cheese
- Salt and pepper to taste
- Fresh basil leaves (for garnish)

Instructions:
1. Set the oven's temperature to 375°F (190°C).
2. Trim the stems from the portobello mushrooms and clean them.
3. Arrange the mushrooms on a parchment-lined baking pan.
4. Add salt and pepper to the mushrooms before serving.
5. Combine the basil pesto with the chicken breasts in another bowl to coat them thoroughly.

6. Cook the chicken breasts in a medium-hot skillet until the center is no longer pink. Then shred the cooked chicken after allowing them to cool slightly.
7. Place shredded chicken and mozzarella cheese on top of each portobello mushroom cap.
8. Bake for 12 to 15 minutes in the oven or until the cheese is melted and bubbling.
9. Take them out of the oven, then give them time to cool.
10. Add fresh basil leaves as a garnish.
11. The Portobello Mushrooms Stuffed with Pesto Chicken is a tasty and filling main dish.

STUFFED BELL PEPPERS WITH GROUND TURKEY AND CAULIFLOWER RICE

Ingredients:
- 4 bell peppers (any color)
- 1 pound ground turkey
- 1 small onion, diced
- 2 cloves garlic, minced
- 1 cup cauliflower rice
- 1 cup tomato sauce
- 1 teaspoon dried basil
- 1 teaspoon dried oregano
- Salt and pepper to taste
- Shredded mozzarella cheese (optional for topping)
- Fresh parsley (for garnish)

Instructions:
1. Set the oven's temperature to 375°F (190°C).
2. Cut off the bell peppers' tops, then scoop out the seeds and membranes.
3. In a skillet over medium heat, brown the ground turkey until it is no longer pink. Use a wooden spoon to cut it into smaller pieces.

4. Include the cooked turkey in the skillet, along with the minced garlic and onion. Sauté the onion until it turns translucent.
5. Fill the skillet with the tomato sauce, dried basil, oregano, salt, and pepper. To blend, thoroughly stir.
6. Allow the ingredients to melt together by simmering the mixture for 5-7 minutes.
7. Stuff the ground turkey and cauliflower rice into each bell pepper.
8. Put the bell peppers in a baking dish after being stuffed. If preferred, top each pepper with shredded mozzarella cheese.
9. Bake for 25 to 30 minutes in a preheated oven or until the cheese is melted and bubbling and the bell peppers are soft.
10. Take them out of the oven and give them a brief cooling period before serving.
11. Add fresh parsley as a garnish.
12. As a filling and savory main dish, serve the stuffed bell peppers with ground turkey and cauliflower rice.

CHICKEN PICCATA WITH ZUCCHINI NOODLES

Ingredients:
- 2 boneless, skinless chicken breasts pounded to an even thickness
- Salt and pepper to taste
- 1/4 cup all-purpose flour (or almond flour for a gluten-free option)
- 2 tablespoons olive oil
- 2 cloves garlic, minced
- 1/2 cup chicken broth
- 1/4 cup fresh lemon juice
- 2 tablespoons capers
- 2 tablespoons unsalted butter

- 2 medium zucchini, spiralized into noodles
- Fresh parsley (for garnish)

Instructions:

1. Add salt and pepper to the chicken breasts.
2. Using flour, coat the chicken breasts and shake off any excess.
3. A giant skillet with medium-high heat is used to heat the olive oil. The chicken breasts should cook thoroughly and turn golden brown on each side after 4-5 minutes. Take out of the skillet, then set it aside.
4. Add the minced garlic to the same skillet and sauté until fragrant.
5. Add the fresh lemon juice and chicken broth. To get rid of any burnt parts, scrape the skillet bottom.
6. After the sauce has been slightly reduced, add the capers and heat for a few minutes.
7. Add the butter and stir until it has completely melted and mixed into the sauce.
8. Add the sauce to the skillet with the cooked chicken breasts.
9. In a different skillet, cook the zucchini noodles for 2 to 3 minutes or until they soften.
10. Distribute the zucchini noodles among the serving plates, then top each with a chicken breast and some sauce.
11. Add fresh parsley as a garnish.
12. As a savory main dish, serve the Chicken Piccata with Zucchini Noodles.

BACON-WRAPPED SCALLOPS WITH ASPARAGUS

Ingredients:
- 12 large scallops
- 12 slices of bacon
- 12 asparagus spears
- Salt and pepper to taste
- Olive oil (for drizzling)
- Lemon wedges (for serving)

Instructions:
1. Set the oven's temperature to 400°F (200°C).
2. Place a piece of bacon around each scallop and fasten it with a toothpick.
3. Arrange the scallops with bacon on a baking pan.
4. Combine the asparagus spears with salt, pepper, and olive oil.
5. On the baking sheet, arrange the asparagus around the scallops.
6. Add a bit extra olive oil to the asparagus and scallops.
7. Bake for 15 to 20 minutes in a preheated oven or until the bacon is crisp and the scallops are done.
8. Take them out of the range and give them a minute to cool.
9. Place lemon wedges on the side to squeeze over the bacon-wrapped scallops and asparagus.
10. Savor this delectable starter or main dish!

GREEK CHICKEN WITH ROASTED VEGETABLES

Ingredients:
- 4 boneless, skinless chicken breasts
- 2 tablespoons olive oil
- 2 tablespoons lemon juice
- 2 cloves garlic, minced
- 1 teaspoon dried oregano
- 1 teaspoon dried basil
- Salt and pepper to taste
- 1 large red bell pepper, sliced
- 1 large yellow bell pepper, sliced
- 1 medium red onion, sliced
- 1 zucchini, sliced
- 1 cup cherry tomatoes
- Crumbled feta cheese (for serving)
- Fresh parsley (for garnish)

Instructions:
1. Set the oven's temperature to 425°F (220°C).
2. In a bowl, combine the olive oil, lemon juice, minced garlic, dried oregano, basil, salt, and pepper to make a marinade.
3. Arrange the chicken breasts in a baking dish and cover them completely with the marinade. Allow them to marinade in the refrigerator overnight or for at least 30 minutes.
4. Place the cherry tomatoes, red onion, zucchini, and bell pepper slices in a different baking dish.
5. Add some olive oil and salt and pepper to the vegetables.
6. Put both of the baking trays in the preheated oven. Roast the vegetables for about 15-20 minutes, until soft, and bake the chicken for about 20-25 minutes, or until cooked.
7. Take the chicken and veggies out of the oven and give them a moment to cool.

8. Garnish the roasted vegetables with fresh parsley and crumbled feta cheese before serving the Greek chicken.
9. Delight in this rich and wholesome supper!

SALMON AND SPINACH QUICHE

Ingredients:
- 1 prepared pie crust
- 6 ounces salmon fillet, cooked and flaked
- 2 cups fresh spinach, chopped
- 1/2 cup grated Gruyere cheese
- 4 large eggs
- 1 cup milk
- 1/4 teaspoon salt
- 1/4 teaspoon black pepper
- 1/4 teaspoon dried dill (optional)

Instructions:
1. Set the oven's temperature to 375°F (190°C).
2. After rolling out the pie dough as directed, press it into a pie dish and cut the excess.
3. Sauté the spinach in a skillet until it wilts. Take it off the stove and let it cool.
4. Cover the bottom of the pie crust equally with the cooked and flaked salmon.
5. Top the salmon with the sautéed spinach and grated Gruyere cheese.
6. Combine the eggs, milk, salt, pepper, and dried dill (if using) in a bowl.
7. Fill the pie shell with the salmon, spinach, and cheese. Then, pour the egg mixture on top.
8. Bake the quiche in the oven for 35 to 40 minutes until the top is golden brown and the middle is set.
9. Take it out of the range, then let it cool a little before cutting.
10. Make the salmon and spinach quiche and serve it for a beautiful and filling meal for breakfast, brunch, or lunch.

SPICY SHRIMP AND ZUCCHINI NOODLES

Ingredients:
- 1 pound shrimp, peeled and deveined
- 2 medium zucchini, spiralized into noodles
- 2 tablespoons olive oil
- 3 cloves garlic, minced
- 1/4 teaspoon red pepper flakes (adjust to taste)
- Salt and pepper to taste
- Juice of 1/2 lemon
- Fresh parsley (for garnish)

Instructions:
1. In a big skillet over medium heat, warm the olive oil.
2. Add the red pepper flakes and minced garlic to the skillet. Sauté until aromatic for about a minute.
3. Add the shrimp to the skillet and cook for two to three minutes on each side or until pink and fully cooked. Add salt and pepper to taste.
4. Take the cooked shrimp out of the pan and place them aside.
5. Include the spiralized zucchini noodles in the same skillet. Sauté the noodles for two to three minutes or until they soften.
6. Add the cooked shrimp and zucchini noodles back to the skillet.
7. Drizzle the shrimp and noodles with the lemon juice, then toss to mix.
8. If necessary, add more salt and pepper to the dish.
9. Add fresh parsley as a garnish.
10. As a tasty, low-carb main dish, offer spicy shrimp and zucchini noodles.

ASIAN BEEF LETTUCE WRAPS

Ingredients:
- 1 pound ground beef
- 2 tablespoons soy sauce
- 1 tablespoon hoisin sauce
- 1 tablespoon sesame oil
- 2 cloves garlic, minced
- 1 teaspoon fresh ginger, grated
- 1/2 teaspoon red pepper flakes (optional)
- 1 cup shredded carrots
- 1/2 cup sliced green onions
- 1/4 cup chopped fresh cilantro
- Butter lettuce leaves (for wrapping)

Instructions:
1. Over medium heat, sauté the ground beef in a skillet until it is browned and cooked. Remove any extra fat.
2. Combine the soy sauce, hoisin sauce, sesame oil, grated ginger, chopped garlic, and red pepper flakes (if using) in a small bowl.
3. To the cooked ground beef in the skillet, add the sauce mixture. To thoroughly coat the meat, stir.
4. Fill the skillet with the shredded carrots, thinly sliced green onions, and chopped cilantro. To blend, stir.
5. Cook the vegetables for an additional 2 to 3 minutes or until they start to soften.
6. Turn off the heat and let the mixture to cool gradually.
7. To make lettuce wraps, spoon the beef mixture onto butter lettuce leaves.
8. Offer the Asian Beef Lettuce Wraps as a flavorful and savory dinner or starter.

CHICKEN CORDON BLEU CASSEROLE

Ingredients:
- 4 boneless, skinless chicken breasts
- Salt and pepper to taste
- 8 slices ham
- 8 slices Swiss cheese
- 1 cup panko breadcrumbs
- 1/4 cup grated Parmesan cheese
- 2 tablespoons melted butter
- 1/2 cup chicken broth
- 1/2 cup heavy cream

Instructions:
1. Set the oven's temperature to 375°F (190°C).
2. Add salt and pepper to the chicken breasts.
3. Put the chicken breasts in an oven-safe dish.
4. Top each chicken breast with two slices of Swiss cheese and two slices of ham.
5. Mix the melted butter, grated Parmesan cheese, and panko breadcrumbs in a separate bowl. Mix thoroughly.
6. Cover the chicken breasts evenly with the breadcrumb mixture.
7. Fill the baking dish's bottom with the heavy cream and chicken broth.
8. Bake for 25 to 30 minutes in a preheated oven or until the chicken is done and the breadcrumbs are golden.
9. Take it out of the range, then allow it to cool before serving.
10. As a delectable and soothing main dish, serve the Chicken Cordon Bleu Casserole.

BAKED LEMON HERB COD WITH GREEN BEANS

Ingredients:
- 4 cod fillets
- Salt and pepper to taste
- 2 tablespoons olive oil
- 2 tablespoons lemon juice
- 1 tablespoon minced fresh parsley
- 1 teaspoon chopped fresh thyme
- 1 teaspoon chopped fresh rosemary
- 1 pound green beans, trimmed
- Lemon wedges (for serving)

Instructions:
1. Set the oven's temperature to 400°F (200°C).
2. Salt and pepper the cod fillets on both sides.
3. In a small bowl, combine the olive oil, lemon juice, minced parsley, thyme, and rosemary to make a marinade.
4. Arrange the cod fillets in a baking dish and cover them with the marinade, ensuring they are completely protected.
5. In the baking dish, position the green beans around the fish fillets.
6. Add salt and pepper to the green beans and drizzle olive oil.
7. Bake in the preheated oven for 12 to 15 minutes, or until the green beans are soft and the cod is opaque and flakes readily with a fork.
8. Take it out of the oven, then give it some time to cool.
9. Put lemon wedges on the side to squeeze over the baked lemon herb cod and green beans.
10. Savor this tasty and light seafood meal!

GRILLED EGGPLANT PARMESAN

Ingredients:
- 2 large eggplants, sliced lengthwise into 1/4-inch thick slices
- Olive oil (for brushing)
- Salt and pepper to taste
- 2 cups marinara sauce
- 2 cups shredded mozzarella cheese
- 1/2 cup grated Parmesan cheese
- Fresh basil leaves (for garnish)

Instructions:
1. Set the grill to a medium-high temperature.
2. Sprinkle salt and pepper over the eggplant slices after brushing them with olive oil.
3. Grill the slices of eggplant for two to three minutes on each side or until they are soft and have grill marks.
4. Take the grilled eggplant slices off and give them a few minutes to cool.
5. Set the oven's temperature to 375°F (190°C).
6. Place a thin layer of marinara sauce on the bottom of a baking dish.
7. Spread grilled eggplant slices in a layer on top of the marinara sauce.
8. Top the eggplant pieces with grated Parmesan cheese and shredded mozzarella cheese.
9. Continue layering the cheese, eggplant pieces, and marinara sauce until all ingredients have been used.
10. Bake in the oven for 20 to 25 minutes, or until the cheese is melted and bubbling.
11. Take it out of the range and allow it to cool before serving.
12. Add fresh basil leaves as a garnish.
13. Make the Grilled Eggplant Parmesan into a delectable vegetarian main dish.

CAULIFLOWER PIZZA WITH CHICKEN AND PESTO

Ingredients: For the cauliflower crust:
- 1 large head cauliflower, riced
- 1/2 cup shredded mozzarella cheese
- 1/4 cup grated Parmesan cheese
- 1/2 teaspoon dried oregano
- 1/2 teaspoon garlic powder
- 2 large eggs
- Salt and pepper to taste

For the toppings:

- 1/2 cup basil pesto
- 1 cup cooked chicken breast, shredded
- 1 cup shredded mozzarella cheese
- Cherry tomatoes, halved
- Fresh basil leaves (for garnish)

Instructions:
1. Set the oven's temperature to 425°F (220°C).
2. In a microwave-safe bowl, add the riced cauliflower and cook for 5 minutes on high. Allow it to cool a little.
3. Squeeze as much liquid as possible from the cooked cauliflower by placing it on a fresh kitchen towel.
4. Combine the cauliflower, eggs, shredded mozzarella cheese, grated Parmesan cheese, dried oregano, salt, and pepper in a mixing dish. Mix thoroughly until doughlike consistency develops.
5. Cover a baking sheet with parchment paper after spreading the cauliflower mixture to create a circular pizza crust.
6. Bake the cauliflower crust for 15 to 20 minutes or until it is firm and golden brown.
7. Take the crust out of the oven and give it a minute to cool.

8. Cover the crust evenly with the basil pesto, leaving a thin border.
9. Sprinkle shredded chicken, mozzarella cheese, and cherry tomato halves on the pesto.
10. Put the pizza back in the oven and cook it for 10-15 minutes or until the cheese is melted and bubbling.
11. Take it out of the oven and give it some time to cool.
12. Add fresh basil leaves as a garnish.
13. As a healthy option to regular pizza, offer the Cauliflower Pizza with Chicken and Pesto.

SKILLET PORK CHOPS WITH CABBAGE AND APPLES

Ingredients:
- 4 boneless pork chops
- Salt and pepper to taste
- 2 tablespoons olive oil
- 1 small head of cabbage, thinly sliced
- 2 apples, cored and sliced
- 1 onion, sliced
- 2 cloves garlic, minced
- 1 teaspoon dried thyme
- 1/2 cup chicken broth
- 2 tablespoons apple cider vinegar
- Fresh parsley (for garnish)

Instructions:
1. Sprinkle salt and pepper over both sides of the pork chops.
2. In a skillet over medium-high heat, warm the olive oil.
3. Place the pork chops in the skillet and cook for 4-5 minutes on each side or until browned and done. Take out of the skillet, then set it aside.

4. Combine the sliced cabbage, apples, onion, minced garlic, and dry thyme in the same skillet. The cabbage should start to soften after around 5 minutes of sautéing.
5. Add the apple cider vinegar and chicken broth. To blend, thoroughly stir.
6. Place the finished pork chops back into the skillet with the cabbage mixture.
7. Lower the heat to a low setting, cover the skillet, and simmer the mixture for 10 to 15 minutes until the cabbage is soft and the flavors are well blended.
8. Turn off the heat and give the skillet some time to cool.
9. Add fresh parsley as a garnish.

STUFFED TOMATOES WITH GROUND CHICKEN AND SPINACH

Ingredients:
- 4 large tomatoes
- 1 pound ground chicken
- 1 small onion, finely chopped
- 2 cloves garlic, minced
- 2 cups fresh spinach, chopped
- 1/2 cup grated Parmesan cheese
- 1/4 cup bread crumbs (or almond flour for a low-carb option)
- 1 tablespoon chopped fresh basil
- 1 tablespoon chopped fresh parsley
- Salt and pepper to taste

Instructions:

1. Set the oven's temperature to 375°F (190°C).
2. Cut each tomato's top off, then scoop the pulp and seeds to create hollow shells. Place aside.
3. In a skillet over medium heat, brown the ground chicken until it is no longer pink. Use a wooden spoon to cut it into smaller pieces.

4. Combine the chicken in the skillet with the minced garlic and finely chopped onion. Sauté the onion until it turns translucent.
5. Stir in the spinach and heat it in the skillet until it wilts.
6. Turn off the heat and let the mixture to cool gradually.
7. Combine the cooked chicken and spinach mixture in a bowl with the bread crumbs, grated Parmesan cheese, fresh basil, parsley, salt, and pepper. Mix thoroughly.
8. Fill each hollow tomato with the chicken and spinach mixture by gently pressing it down.
9. Arrange the stuffed tomatoes in a baking dish and heat the filling and tomatoes in a preheated oven for 20 to 25 minutes.
10. Take them out of the oven and allow them to cool before serving.
11. Present the stuffed tomatoes as a tasty and wholesome main dish. They go well with ground chicken and spinach.

STEAK AND VEGGIE STIR-FRY

Ingredients:
- 1 pound steak (such as sirloin or flank), thinly sliced
- 2 tablespoons soy sauce
- 1 tablespoon oyster sauce
- 1 tablespoon cornstarch
- 1 tablespoon sesame oil
- 2 tablespoons vegetable oil
- 1 red bell pepper, sliced
- 1 green bell pepper, sliced
- 1 medium onion, sliced
- 2 cups broccoli florets
- 2 cloves garlic, minced
- Salt and pepper to taste

Instructions:

1. Mix the sesame oil, cornstarch, oyster sauce, and soy sauce in a bowl. To make a marinade, thoroughly combine.
2. Add the steak slices to the marinade, and let them sit for 15 to 20 minutes.
3. In a sizable skillet or wok, heat vegetable oil over high heat.
4. Place the steak in the skillet after marinating, and cook for 2–3 minutes or until browned. Take out of the skillet, then set it aside.
5. Include broccoli florets, onion, bell pepper slices, and minced garlic in the same skillet. Cook the vegetables in a stir-fry for 3–4 minutes or until they are crisp and tender.
6. Add the cooked steak and vegetables back to the skillet. To blend the flavors, stir-fry for a further 1-2 minutes.
7. To taste, add salt and pepper to the dish.
8. Take it off the fire and give it a few minutes to cool.
9. Present the steak and vegetables. Stir-fry is a delectable and filling main dish.

BAKED GREEK-STYLE SHRIMP WITH TOMATOES AND FETA

Ingredients:
- 1 pound shrimp, peeled and deveined
- 2 tablespoons olive oil
- 4 cloves garlic, minced
- 1 teaspoon dried oregano
- 1/2 teaspoon dried basil
- 1/4 teaspoon red pepper flakes (adjust to taste)
- 1 cup cherry tomatoes, halved
- 1/2 cup crumbled feta cheese
- Fresh parsley (for garnish)
- Lemon wedges (for serving)

Instructions:

1. Set the oven's temperature to 425°F (220°C).
2. Combine the shrimp with olive oil, minced garlic, dried oregano, dried basil, and red pepper flakes in a baking dish. Ensure that the shrimp are well coated.
3. Place the cherry tomato halves in the baking dish and combine them delicately with the shrimp.
4. Bake the shrimp in the oven for 10 to 12 minutes or until they are cooked and pink.
5. Remove from the oven, then top the shrimp and tomatoes with feta cheese crumbles.
6. Place the baking dish in the oven for 2 to 3 minutes or until the feta cheese is soft.
7. Take it out of the oven, then set it aside to cool.
8. Add fresh parsley as a garnish.
9. Put lemon wedges on the side to squeeze over the baked Greek-style shrimp with tomatoes and feta.
10. Savor this savory and wonderful seafood dish!

CHICKEN AND GREEN BEAN STIR-FRY

Ingredients:
- 1 pound boneless, skinless chicken breasts sliced into thin strips
- 2 tablespoons soy sauce
- 1 tablespoon oyster sauce
- 1 tablespoon cornstarch
- 2 tablespoons vegetable oil
- 1 pound green beans, trimmed and cut into bite-sized pieces
- 2 cloves garlic, minced
- 1 teaspoon grated fresh ginger
- Salt and pepper to taste
- Sesame seeds (for garnish)

Instructions:
1. Mix the cornstarch, oyster sauce, and soy sauce in a bowl. To make a sauce, thoroughly combine.

2. Add the sauce to the chicken slices and let them marinate for 15 to 20 minutes.
3. In a sizable skillet or wok, heat vegetable oil over high heat.
4. Stir-fry the chicken in the skillet after it marries for about 5 to 6 minutes or until it is cooked through and browned. Take out of the skillet, then set it aside.
5. Add the green beans, minced garlic, and grated ginger in the same skillet. The green beans should be soft but crisp after 3–4 minutes of stirring.
6. Add the cooked chicken and green beans back to the skillet. To blend the flavors, stir-fry for a further 1-2 minutes.
7. To taste, add salt and pepper to the dish.
8. Take it off the fire and give it a few minutes to cool.
9. Add sesame seeds as a garnish.
10. Present the Chicken and Green Bean Stir-Fry as a tasty and nutritious main dish.

MOROCCAN CHICKEN WITH CAULIFLOWER COUSCOUS

Ingredients: For the chicken:
- 4 boneless, skinless chicken breasts
- 2 tablespoons olive oil
- 2 cloves garlic, minced
- 2 teaspoons ground cumin
- 2 teaspoons ground coriander
- 1 teaspoon ground paprika
- 1/2 teaspoon ground cinnamon
- Salt and pepper to taste

For the cauliflower couscous:

- 1 head cauliflower, grated or processed into a couscous-like texture
- 2 tablespoons olive oil

- 1 small onion, finely chopped
- 2 cloves garlic, minced
- 1 teaspoon ground cumin
- 1 teaspoon ground coriander
- Salt and pepper to taste
- Fresh cilantro (for garnish)

Instructions:

1. Set the oven's temperature to 375°F (190°C).
2. To make a spice combination, combine the minced garlic, ground cumin, coriander, paprika, cinnamon, salt, and pepper in a small bowl.
3. Evenly rub the spice mixture into the chicken breasts to coat them.
4. In an oven-safe skillet, heat the olive oil over medium-high heat.
5. Place the chicken breasts in the skillet and brown them on each side for 2 to 3 minutes.
6. Place the skillet in the hot oven and bake for 15 to 20 minutes, or until the chicken is cooked and the middle is no longer pink.
7. Make the cauliflower couscous while the chicken is cooking.
8. In a separate skillet, heat the olive oil over medium heat.
9. Stir in the minced garlic and finely diced onion in the skillet. Sauté the onion until it turns translucent.
10. Stir in the grated cauliflower and cook for 5 to 6 minutes or until cooked.
11. Add the salt, pepper, ground cumin, and ground coriander. To integrate the flavors, thoroughly mix.
12. Take it off the stove and let it cool just a little.
13. Top the cauliflower couscous with fresh cilantro and serve it with the Moroccan chicken.

SAUSAGE, KALE, AND CAULIFLOWER SOUP

Ingredients:
- 1 tablespoon olive oil
- 1 pound sausage (such as Italian or chorizo), casings removed
- 1 onion, diced
- 3 cloves garlic, minced
- 4 cups chicken broth
- 1 head cauliflower, cut into small florets
- 2 cups chopped kale
- 1 teaspoon dried thyme
- Salt and pepper to taste
- Fresh parsley (for garnish)

Instructions:

1. Heat the olive oil over medium heat in a big pot or Dutch oven.
2. Add the sausage to the pot and simmer, crumbling it with a spoon as it cooks until browned.
3. Stir in the diced onion and cook it in the pot until it is transparent.
4. Add the minced garlic and stir. Cook for an additional minute.
5. Add the chicken broth and boil the mixture.
6. Fill the saucepan with the chopped kale, dried thyme, salt, and pepper. Also, add the cauliflower florets. To blend, thoroughly stir.
7. Once the cauliflower is cooked and the flavors are blended, turn the heat down to low, cover the pot, and simmer for 20 to 25 minutes.
8. Take it off the fire and give it a few minutes to cool.
9. Add fresh parsley as a garnish.
10. Dish out the sausage.

CHICKEN, BACON, AND AVOCADO SALAD WITH CREAMY DRESSING

Ingredients: For the salad:
- 4 cups mixed salad greens
- 2 cups cooked chicken breast, shredded or diced
- 4 slices cooked bacon, crumbled
- 1 avocado, sliced
- Cherry tomatoes, halved
- Red onion, thinly sliced
- Crumbled feta cheese (optional)
- Chopped fresh parsley (for garnish)

For the creamy dressing:

- 1/4 cup mayonnaise
- 1/4 cup Greek yogurt
- 1 tablespoon Dijon mustard
- 1 tablespoon lemon juice
- 1 clove garlic, minced
- Salt and pepper to taste

Instructions:

1. Toss the mixed salad greens, cooked chicken breast, bacon bits, cherry tomatoes, red onion, avocado slices, and crumbled feta cheese (if using) in a large salad bowl.
2. To make the creamy dressing, combine the mayonnaise, Greek yogurt, Dijon mustard, lemon juice, minced garlic, salt, and pepper in a separate small bowl.
3. In the big salad bowl with the salad items, drizzle the creamy dressing over everything. Gently toss everything to distribute the sauce evenly.
4. Add freshly chopped parsley to the salad as a garnish.
5. As a tasty and filling lunch, serve the Chicken, Bacon, and Avocado Salad with Creamy Dressing.

LEMON HERB BAKED HALIBUT

Ingredients:
- 4 halibut fillets
- 2 tablespoons olive oil
- Zest of 1 lemon
- Juice of 1 lemon
- 2 cloves garlic, minced
- 1 tablespoon chopped fresh parsley
- 1 teaspoon chopped fresh thyme
- Salt and pepper to taste
- Lemon slices (for serving)

Instructions:
1. Set the oven's temperature to 400°F (200°C).
2. The halibut fillets should be placed in a baking dish.
3. To make a marinade, combine the olive oil, lemon zest, lemon juice, minced garlic, fresh parsley, thyme, salt, and pepper in a small bowl.
4. After thoroughly coating the halibut fillets, pour the marinade over them.
5. Give the halibut fillets around 15 to 20 minutes to marinade.
6. When the halibut is opaque and flakes readily with a fork, bake it in the oven for 12 to 15 minutes.
7. Take it out of the oven, then set it aside to cool.
8. Put lemon slices on the side to squeeze over the fish as you serve the Lemon Herb Baked Halibut.
9. Savor this tasty and nutritious seafood dish!

SPAGHETTI SQUASH AND MEAT SAUCE

Ingredients:
- 1 medium spaghetti squash
- 1 pound of ground meat (such as beef or turkey)
- 1 small onion, diced
- 2 cloves garlic, minced
- 1 can (14 ounces) crushed tomatoes
- 1 can (6 ounces) tomato paste
- 1 teaspoon dried oregano
- 1 teaspoon dried basil
- Salt and pepper to taste
- Fresh parsley (for garnish)
- Grated Parmesan cheese (optional)

Instructions:
1. Set the oven's temperature to 400°F (200°C).
2. Remove the seeds from the spaghetti squash by cutting it in half lengthwise.
3. Lay the spaghetti squash halves, cut side down, on a baking sheet.
4. Bake in the preheated oven for 40 to 45 minutes, or until the squash is soft and the strands are readily scraped with a fork.
5. Make the beef sauce while the spaghetti squash bakes.
6. In a skillet over medium heat, sauté the ground beef until it is cooked and browned. Remove any extra fat.
7. Combine the cooked meat in the skillet with the minced garlic and onion. Sauté the onion until it turns translucent.
8. Add salt, pepper, dried oregano, dried basil, tomato paste, and smashed tomatoes. Blend thoroughly.
9. Simmer the beef sauce for 15 to 20 minutes to allow the flavors to blend.
10. After the spaghetti squash has finished cooking, kindly take it out of the oven and let it cool.

11. To make spaghetti-like strands, scrape the spaghetti squash's flesh with a fork.
12. Distribute the spaghetti squash strands between dishes or serving plates.
13. Drizzle the spaghetti squash with the beef sauce.
14. If wanted, garnish with freshly chopped parsley and grated Parmesan cheese.
15. As a delightful low-carb substitute for regular spaghetti and meat sauce, serve the spaghetti squash and meat sauce.

LOW-CARB CHICKEN POT PIE

Ingredients: For the crust:
- 2 cups almond flour
- 1/2 teaspoon salt
- 1/4 cup cold unsalted butter, cubed
- 1 large egg

For the filling:

- 2 tablespoons olive oil
- 1 small onion, diced
- 2 cloves garlic, minced
- 2 medium carrots, diced
- 2 stalks of celery, diced
- 1 cup cauliflower florets, chopped
- 1/2 teaspoon dried thyme
- 1/2 teaspoon dried rosemary
- Salt and pepper to taste
- 2 cups cooked chicken breast, diced
- 1 cup chicken broth
- 1/2 cup heavy cream
- 2 tablespoons cream cheese

Instructions:

1. Set the oven's temperature to 375°F (190°C).

2. Combine salt and almond flour in a mixing basin. When the flour mixture resembles coarse crumbs, combine the cold butter cubes with a pastry cutter or fork.
3. Stir in the egg and continue to mix until the dough comes together.
4. Form an even crust by pressing the dough onto a 9-inch pie plate. Place aside.
5. Set a large skillet over medium heat and warm the olive oil. Cook until the onion is transparent after adding the diced onion and garlic.
6. Include the diced cauliflower, celery, and carrots in the skillet. Cook the vegetables for about 5 minutes or until they begin to soften.
7. Add the salt, pepper, dry rosemary, and dried thyme. Cook for a further two minutes.
8. Stir the veggies and diced chicken together in the skillet.
9. Thoroughly combine the cream cheese, heavy cream, and chicken broth in a small bowl. Fill the skillet with the mixture and add the chicken and vegetables. To blend, stir.
10. It should slightly thicken after cooking the filling for 5 to 7 minutes.
11. Spoon the filling into the prepared pie crust and distribute it evenly.
12. Bake for 20 to 25 minutes in a preheated oven or until the filling is bubbling and the crust is brown.
13. Take it out of the range, then allow it to cool before serving.
14. Make Low Carb Chicken Pot Pie serve as a hearty and delectable supper.

TOFU AND VEGETABLE CURRY

Ingredients:
- 1 block of firm tofu, drained and cubed
- 2 tablespoons vegetable oil
- 1 onion, thinly sliced
- 2 cloves garlic, minced
- 1 tablespoon grated ginger
- 1 bell pepper, thinly sliced
- 1 carrot, thinly sliced
- 1 zucchini, thinly sliced
- 1 can (14 ounces) of coconut milk
- 2 tablespoons red curry paste
- 1 tablespoon soy sauce
- 1 tablespoon lime juice
- 1 tablespoon brown sugar (optional)
- Fresh cilantro (for garnish)
- Cooked rice or naan bread (for serving)

Instructions:
1. In a sizable skillet or wok, heat vegetable oil over medium heat.
2. Include the tofu cubes and fry them in the skillet until they are evenly golden brown. Take out of the skillet, then set it aside.
3. Include the minced garlic, grated ginger, and onion slices in the same skillet. Sauté the onion until it turns translucent.
4. Include the zucchini, carrot, and bell pepper in the skillet. Stir-fry the vegetables for a few minutes or until they begin to soften.
5. Combine the coconut milk, red curry paste, soy sauce, lime juice, and brown sugar (if using) in a small bowl.
6. Pour the coconut milk concoction over the vegetables in the skillet. To blend, thoroughly stir.

7. Return the cooked tofu cubes to the pan and simmer for 10 minutes to let the flavors combine, and the vegetables finish cooking.
8. Take it off the fire and give it a few minutes to cool.
9. Add fresh cilantro as a garnish.
10. Alternatively, serve the tofu and vegetable curry over naan bread and boiled rice.

BAKED CHICKEN PARMESAN WITH ZUCCHINI NOODLES

Ingredients:
- 2 boneless, skinless chicken breasts
- Salt and pepper to taste
- 1/2 cup almond flour
- 1/4 cup grated Parmesan cheese
- 1 teaspoon dried oregano
- 1 teaspoon dried basil
- 1 egg, beaten
- 2 tablespoons olive oil
- 1 cup marinara sauce
- 2 medium zucchini
- Fresh basil leaves (for garnish)

Instructions:
1. Set the oven's temperature to 375°F (190°C).
2. Sprinkle salt and pepper on both sides of the chicken breasts.
3. Mix the almond flour, grated Parmesan cheese, dried oregano, and dried basil in a shallow bowl.
4. Coat each chicken breast in the almond flour mixture, pressing it onto the chicken to help it stick, and then dip it into the beaten egg, letting any excess drip off.
5. In an oven-safe skillet, heat the olive oil over medium-high heat.

6. Add the chicken breasts coated to the skillet and cook for 2 to 3 minutes on each side or until browned.
7. Turn off the heat and evenly spread the marinara sauce over the chicken breasts in the skillet.
8. Place the skillet in the hot oven and bake for 20 to 25 minutes, or until the chicken is cooked and the middle is no longer pink.
9. Make the zucchini noodles while the chicken bakes.
10. To make zucchini noodles, slice the zucchini into thin, noodle-like strips using a spiralizer or a vegetable peeler.
11. Add olive oil to a different skillet and heat it over medium heat. When the zucchini noodles are tender-crisp, add them to the skillet and cook for two to three minutes.
12. Turn off the heat and put the skillet to the side.
13. After the chicken has finished cooking, kindly take it out of the oven and let it cool.
14. Arrange the chicken on a tray or platter and garnish with more marinara and fresh basil.
15. Use the zucchini noodles as a low-carb, healthful alternative to spaghetti to serve with the chicken.
16. Take pleasure in your baked chicken parmesan and zucchini noodles!

SHRIMP AND BROCCOLI ALFREDO

Ingredients:
- 8 ounces fettuccine pasta
- 1 tablespoon olive oil
- 1 pound shrimp, peeled and deveined
- 3 cloves garlic, minced
- 2 cups broccoli florets
- 1 cup heavy cream
- 1/2 cup grated Parmesan cheese
- Salt and pepper to taste
- Fresh parsley (for garnish)

Instructions:
1. Prepare the fettuccine pasta as directed on the package until it is al dente. Drain, then set apart.
2. Warm up the olive oil in a sizable skillet over medium heat.
3. Add the shrimp to the skillet and cook for two to three minutes per side or until pink and fully cooked. Please remove the cooked shrimp from the skillet and lay them aside.
4. Add the minced garlic to the same skillet and cook until fragrant, about 1 minute.
5. Add the broccoli florets to the skillet and cook, stirring occasionally, for 3 to 4 minutes or until tender-crisp.
6. Lower the heat to a low setting and add the heavy cream. To blend, thoroughly stir.
7. Add the grated Parmesan cheese and stir. Cook for 2 to 3 minutes or until the sauce slightly thickens.
8. To taste, add salt and pepper to the sauce.
9. Reintroduce the cooked shrimp and fettuccine to the skillet. Toss everything together until the sauce is evenly distributed over the pasta and prawns.
10. Take it off the fire and give it some time to cool.
11. Add fresh parsley as a garnish.

12. Present the creamy and delectable Shrimp and Broccoli Alfredo as a pasta meal.

GRILLED TOFU WITH CHIMICHURRI SAUCE

Ingredients: For the tofu:
- 1 block firm tofu, drained and sliced into 1/2-inch thick slices
- 2 tablespoons soy sauce
- 1 tablespoon olive oil

For the chimichurri sauce:

- 1 cup fresh parsley leaves
- 1/4 cup fresh cilantro leaves
- 3 cloves garlic, minced
- 1/4 cup red wine vinegar
- 1/4 cup olive oil
- 1/2 teaspoon dried oregano
- 1/4 teaspoon red pepper flakes (adjust to taste)
- Salt and pepper to taste

Instructions:
1. Start your grill or grill pan by heating it to medium-high.
2. Combine soy sauce and olive oil on a small plate. Slices of tofu should be placed in the container and marinated for ten to fifteen minutes.
3. Make the chimichurri sauce in the meanwhile. Combine the parsley, cilantro, red wine vinegar, olive oil, dried oregano, red pepper flakes, salt, and pepper in a food processor or blender. When everything is thoroughly incorporated, and the herbs are minced, pulse.
4. Grill the marinated tofu slices on each side for 3 to 4 minutes or until grill marks appear and they are thoroughly heated.
5. Take the tofu grilled off the heat and set it aside to cool.

6. Spoon the chimichurri sauce over the tofu that has been cooked.
7. Enjoy the tasty and protein-rich Grilled Tofu with Chimichurri Sauce.

CHICKEN AND ASPARAGUS SHEET PAN DINNER

Ingredients:
- 4 boneless, skinless chicken breasts
- 1 pound asparagus, trimmed
- 2 tablespoons olive oil
- 2 cloves garlic, minced
- 1 teaspoon dried thyme
- 1 teaspoon dried rosemary
- Salt and pepper to taste
- Lemon slices (for serving)

Instructions:
1. Set the oven's temperature to 425°F (220°C).
2. On one side of a sizable baking sheet, arrange the chicken breasts.
3. Place the chicken on the baking sheet and place the trimmed asparagus next to it.
4. Combine the olive oil, minced garlic, dried thyme, rosemary, salt, and pepper in a small bowl.
5. Drizzle the chicken breasts and asparagus with the olive oil mixture, stirring to cover everything.
6. Arrange the chicken and asparagus on the baking pan in a single layer.
7. Bake for 20 to 25 minutes in a preheated oven or until the chicken is cooked through, the asparagus is crisp-tender, and the chicken is no longer pink in the center.
8. Take it out of the oven, then give it some time to cool.

9. Place lemon slices on the side of the Chicken and Asparagus Sheet Pan Dinner so guests can squeeze them over the chicken and vegetables.
10. Savor this quick and delectable one-pan supper!

CAULIFLOWER STEAKS WITH MUSHROOM GRAVY

Ingredients: For the cauliflower steaks:
- 1 large head of cauliflower
- 2 tablespoons olive oil
- 1 teaspoon smoked paprika
- 1/2 teaspoon garlic powder
- Salt and pepper to taste

For the mushroom gravy:

- 8 ounces mushrooms, sliced
- 2 tablespoons butter
- 2 cloves garlic, minced
- 2 tablespoons all-purpose flour (or a gluten-free alternative)
- 1 1/2 cups vegetable broth
- 1/2 cup heavy cream
- 1 teaspoon soy sauce
- 1/2 teaspoon dried thyme
- Salt and pepper to taste
- Fresh parsley (for garnish)

Instructions:
1. Set the oven's temperature to 425°F (220°C).
2. Trim the cauliflower leaves and stalk them while leaving the head alone.
3. Cut the cauliflower into steaks that are 1 inch thick, keeping the core intact to keep the steaks from falling apart.

4. Arrange the cauliflower steaks on a parchment-lined baking pan.
5. Combine the olive oil, smoked paprika, garlic powder, salt, and pepper in a small bowl.
6. Use the olive oil mixture to cover both sides of the cauliflower steaks evenly.
7. Bake the cauliflower steaks for 20 to 25 minutes or until they are soft and the edges are browned.
8. Make the mushroom gravy while the cauliflower steaks bake.
9. Heat the butter in a pan over medium heat.
10. Include the mushroom slices and sauté them in the skillet until they release moisture and soften.
11. Stir in the minced garlic and simmer for a further minute or until fragrant.
12. After adding the flour to the mushrooms, mix them to distribute it uniformly.
13. Slowly pour the vegetable broth while stirring constantly to avoid lumps.
14. Season the skillet with salt, pepper, dried thyme, and heavy cream. To blend, thoroughly mix.
15. Stirring occasionally, keep heating the gravy over medium heat until it reaches the required consistency.
16. Take the cauliflower steaks out of the oven and set them aside to cool.
17. Drizzle plenty of mushroom gravy over the cauliflower steaks before serving.
18. Add fresh parsley as a garnish.
19. Savor the wonderful vegetarian Cauliflower Steaks with Mushroom Gravy.

CHAPTER 5:
RECIPE FOR SNACKS

CAPRESE SALAD SKEWERS

Ingredients:
- Cherry tomatoes
- Fresh mozzarella balls (bocconcini)
- Fresh basil leaves
- Balsamic glaze
- Extra-virgin olive oil
- Salt and pepper to taste
- Wooden skewers

Instructions:
1. Thread a cherry tomato, fresh basil leaf, and mozzarella ball onto a wooden skewer.
2. Carry on in this manner until you have the required quantity of skewers.
3. Position the skewers on a plate for serving.
4. Drizzle extra virgin olive oil and balsamic glaze over the skewers.
5. To taste, add salt and pepper to the food.
6. Present the Caprese Salad Skewers to guests as a tasty starter or side dish.

PARMESAN CRISPS WITH PROSCIUTTO AND BASIL

Ingredients:
- 1 cup grated Parmesan cheese
- Thinly sliced prosciutto
- Fresh basil leaves

Instructions:

1. Set the oven's temperature to 400°F (200°C).
2. Use parchment paper to cover a baking sheet.
3. Leaving room between each mound, spoon little piles of grated Parmesan cheese onto the prepared baking sheet.
4. To make Parmesan crisps, gently distribute the cheese mounds into thin rings.
5. Bake in the oven for 5-7 minutes or until the cheese has melted and the sides are golden brown.
6. Take the Parmesan crisps out of the range and allow them to cool completely.
7. After they have cooled, add a slice of prosciutto and a basil leaf to each Parmesan crisp.
8. As a classy starter, offer the Parmesan Crisps with Prosciutto and Basil.

GREEK SALAD CUCUMBER BITES

Ingredients:

- English cucumbers
- Cherry tomatoes, halved
- Kalamata olives, pitted and halved
- Feta cheese, crumbled
- Fresh dill, chopped
- Extra-virgin olive oil
- Lemon juice
- Salt and pepper to taste

Instructions:

1. Slice the English cucumbers into 1-inch-thick slices.
2. To make each cucumber slice into a cup-like form, use a melon baller or a spoon to scoop out a tiny hollow in each one.
3. Mix the cherry tomatoes, Kalamata olives, feta cheese crumbles, and fresh dill in a bowl.
4. Add lemon juice and extra virgin olive oil to the mixture.

5. Toss lightly to incorporate after adding salt and pepper to taste.
6. Using a spoon, fill each cucumber cup with the Greek salad mixture.
7. Arrange the cucumber bites from the Greek salad on a serving plate.
8. If desired, add more dill as a garnish.
9. Offer the Greek Salad Cucumber Bites as a light and energizing starter.

SPICED MIXED NUTS

Ingredients:
- 2 cups mixed nuts (such as almonds, cashews, walnuts, and pecans)
- 1 tablespoon olive oil
- 1 tablespoon honey (optional)
- 1 teaspoon ground cumin
- 1/2 teaspoon smoked paprika
- 1/2 teaspoon garlic powder
- 1/4 teaspoon cayenne pepper (adjust to taste)
- Salt to taste

Instructions:
1. Set the oven's temperature to 350°F (175°C).
2. Combine the mixed nuts, olive oil, honey (if using), salt, cayenne pepper, garlic powder, ground cumin, and smoky paprika in a bowl. Toss thoroughly to evenly coat the nuts.
3. Spread the salted nuts on a baking sheet covered with parchment paper in a single layer.
4. Toasted and aromatic nuts should be baked in a preheated oven for 10 to 15 minutes, stirring once or twice to promote equal browning.
5. Take the spiced mixed nuts out of the oven and allow them to cool completely.

6. After the nuts have cooled, place them in a serving bowl or an airtight container for storage.
7. Offer the spiced mixed nuts to your guests as a tasty and crispy snack.

DEVILED EGGS WITH SMOKED SALMON

Ingredients:
- 6 hard-boiled eggs
- 2 tablespoons mayonnaise
- 1 tablespoon Dijon mustard
- 1 tablespoon fresh dill, chopped
- Salt and pepper to taste
- Smoked salmon, sliced
- Fresh dill sprigs (for garnish)

Instructions:
1. Cut the hard-boiled eggs in half lengthwise after peeling them.
2. Remove the yolks with a spoon and place them in a bowl.
3. Using a fork, mash the egg yolks until they are crumbly.
4. Add mayonnaise, Dijon mustard, finely chopped fresh dill, salt, and pepper to the mashed egg yolks. Well, combine till creamy and smooth.
5. Fill the egg white halves with the yolk mixture using a spoon or a pastry bag.
6. Add a slice of smoked salmon to the top of each deviled egg.
7. Add fresh dill sprigs as a garnish.
8. As a tasty starter, serve the deviled eggs with smoked salmon.

TUNA-STUFFED MINI BELL PEPPERS

Ingredients:
- Mini bell peppers
- 1 can (5 ounces) tuna, drained
- 2 tablespoons mayonnaise
- 1 tablespoon Dijon mustard
- 1/4 cup red onion, finely chopped
- 1/4 cup celery, finely chopped
- 1 tablespoon fresh parsley, chopped
- Salt and pepper to taste

Instructions:
1. Cut the small bell peppers' tops off and scoop out the seeds and membranes.
2. Combine the drained tuna, mayonnaise, Dijon mustard, celery, red onion, and fresh parsley in a bowl. Season with salt and pepper. Blend thoroughly.
3. Fill each miniature bell pepper with the tuna mixture.
4. Position the filled tiny bell peppers on a serving plate.
5. Put the mixture in the fridge for at least 30 minutes to let the flavors merge and the peppers cool.
6. Offer the tuna-stuffed little bell peppers as a delicious and eye-catching appetizer.

CELERY STICKS WITH ALMOND BUTTER

Ingredients:
- Celery stalks
- Almond butter

Instructions:
1. After washing, trim the celery stalks to workable lengths of 3 to 4 inches.
2. Cover the groove in the middle of each celery stick with almond butter.

3. Offer the crunchy and healthy celery sticks with almond butter as a snack.

TURKEY AND CHEESE ROLL-UPS

Ingredients:
- Deli turkey slices
- Cheese slices (such as cheddar, Swiss, or provolone)
- Mustard or mayonnaise (optional)

Instructions:
1. Place a flat slice of deli turkey on a smooth surface.
2. Top the turkey slice with a piece of cheese.
3. If preferred, smear the cheese with a thin layer of mustard or mayonnaise.
4. Form a cylinder by carefully rolling the cheese and turkey.
5. Repeat with the remaining cheese and turkey slices.
6. Cut each roll-up into small pieces.
7. Offer the Turkey and Cheese Roll-Ups as an easy and delectable starter or snack.

CHEDDAR AND CHIVE CAULIFLOWER BITES

Ingredients:
- 1 small head of cauliflower
- 1 cup shredded cheddar cheese
- 2 tablespoons chopped chives
- 2 eggs
- Salt and pepper to taste

Instructions:
1. Set your oven to 400 degrees Fahrenheit (200 degrees Celsius) and cover a baking sheet with parchment paper.

2. Separate the cauliflower florets, then add them to the food processor. Cauliflower should be pulsed until it resembles rice-like grains.
3. Place the cauliflower in a bowl that can be placed in the microwave and cook for 4-5 minutes or until it is soft.
4. Squeeze out as much liquid as possible from the cooked cauliflower by placing it in a fresh kitchen towel or cheesecloth.
5. Combine the cauliflower, shredded cheddar cheese, chives, eggs, salt, and pepper in a mixing bowl. Blend thoroughly.
6. Form the mixture into bite-sized patties using your hands, then arrange them on the lined baking sheet.
7. Bake the bites in the oven for 15 to 20 minutes or until crispy and golden brown.
8. Take them out of the oven and allow them to cool before serving.
9. Offer the low-carb Cheddar and Chive Cauliflower Bites as a tasty appetizer or snack.

ZUCCHINI PIZZA BITES

Ingredients:
- 2 medium zucchini
- 1/2 cup marinara sauce
- 1/2 cup shredded mozzarella cheese
- Mini pepperoni slices (optional)
- Dried oregano (for sprinkling)

Instructions:
1. Line a baking sheet with parchment paper and preheat your oven to 425°F (220°C).
2. Cut the zucchini into 1/2-inch-thick, thick circles.
3. Arrange the zucchini rounds on the prepared baking sheet and drizzle each with a little marinara sauce.
4. Add shredded mozzarella cheese and little pepperoni slices to the top of each zucchini round.

5. Drizzle dry oregano on top of each ring of zucchini.
6. Bake in the oven for 10 to 12 minutes, or until the cheese is melted and bubbling.
7. Take them out of the range and allow them to cool before serving.
8. Serve the zucchini pizza bites as a healthier alternative to regular pizza bites.

HAM AND CREAM CHEESE CUCUMBER ROLL-UPS

Ingredients:
- English cucumber
- Sliced deli ham
- Cream cheese

Instructions:
1. Cut the English cucumber into long, thin strips using a mandoline slicer or a vegetable peeler.
2. Place a flat slice of deli ham on a clean surface.
3. Top the ham slice with a thin layer of cream cheese.
4. Roll up tightly with a cucumber strip on top of the cream cheese.
5. Repeat with the remaining ham, cream cheese, and cucumber strips.
6. Cut each roll-up into small pieces.
7. Offer the savory, low-carb Ham and Cream Cheese Cucumber Roll-Ups as an appetizer or snack.

COTTAGE CHEESE WITH BERRIES AND NUTS

Ingredients:
- Cottage cheese
- Fresh berries (such as strawberries, blueberries, or raspberries)

- Mixed nuts (such as almonds, walnuts, or pecans), chopped

Instructions:

1. Place cottage cheese in a serving basin or platter.
2. Add a layer of mixed nuts and fresh berries to the cottage cheese.
3. Use cottage cheese with nuts and berries as a healthy, protein-rich snack or light breakfast.

EDAMAME WITH SEA SALT AND LEMON

Ingredients:
- 1 cup frozen edamame, thawed
- Sea salt to taste
- Fresh lemon wedges

Instructions:

1. Add the thawed edamame to a pot of boiling water.
2. To make the edamame tender, cook them for 3 to 5 minutes.
3. Empty the cooked edamame into a serving basin after draining them.
4. Sea salt the edamame and toss to coat thoroughly.
5. Squeeze some fresh lemon juice over the edamame using the lemon wedges.
6. Offer edamame as a wholesome and energizing snack with sea salt and lemon.

ROASTED CHICKPEAS WITH GARLIC AND PARMESAN

Ingredients:
- 1 can (15 ounces) chickpeas (garbanzo beans), rinsed and drained

- 2 tablespoons olive oil
- 2 cloves garlic, minced
- 1/4 cup grated Parmesan cheese
- Salt and pepper to taste

Instructions:

1. Set your oven to 400 degrees Fahrenheit (200 degrees Celsius) and cover a baking sheet with parchment paper.
2. Spread the rinsed, drained chickpeas on the prepared baking sheet and use a paper towel to wipe them dry.
3. Pour olive oil over the chickpeas and toss to distribute it evenly.
4. Top the chickpeas with chopped garlic, grated Parmesan cheese, salt, and pepper. To get a uniform coating, toss one more.
5. Arrange the chickpeas on the baking sheet in a single layer.
6. Bake the chickpeas in the preheated oven for 25 to 30 minutes or until golden and crispy, tossing once or twice to ensure equal browning.
7. Take the roasted chickpeas out of the oven and let them cool fully.
8. As a delightful and protein-rich snack, serve the roasted chickpeas with garlic and parmesan.

MINI CRUSTLESS QUICHE MUFFINS

Ingredients:
- Cooking spray
- 6 large eggs
- 1/4 cup milk
- 1/2 cup shredded cheddar cheese
- 1/4 cup diced ham or cooked bacon
- 1/4 cup diced bell peppers
- 1/4 cup diced onions
- Salt and pepper to taste

- Fresh herbs (such as parsley or chives), chopped (for garnish)

Instructions:

1. Heat your oven to 375°F (190°C) and spray cooking spray in a tiny muffin pan.
2. In a bowl, mix the milk and eggs until thoroughly incorporated.
3. After incorporating the shredded cheddar cheese, add the diced ham or cooked bacon, bell peppers, chopped onions, salt, and pepper.
4. Fill each cup in the oiled mini muffin tin about three-fourths full with the egg mixture.
5. Bake the quiche muffins in the oven for 12 to 15 minutes or until golden and set.
6. Remove the muffins from the muffin tray after they have cooled after being removed from the range.
7. Add fresh herbs as a garnish to the mini crustless quiche muffins.
8. The quiche muffins make a delicious, portable breakfast or snack option. Serve them warm or at room temperature.

SPICY ROASTED PUMPKIN SEEDS

Ingredients:
- Pumpkin seeds (from a pumpkin or pre-packaged)
- 1 tablespoon olive oil
- 1/2 teaspoon chili powder
- 1/4 teaspoon garlic powder
- 1/4 teaspoon paprika
- 1/4 teaspoon salt (adjust to taste)

Instructions:

1. Set a baking sheet on your oven's 350°F (175°C) rack and preheat the oven.

2. Use a paper towel to dry the pumpkin seeds after rinsing them in cold water.
3. Combine the pumpkin seeds, salt, paprika, garlic powder, chili powder, and olive oil in a bowl. Make sure the coating covers the roots evenly.
4. Arrange the spiced pumpkin seeds on the prepared baking sheet in a single layer.
5. Bake the pumpkin seeds in the oven for 10 to 15 minutes or until they are crispy and golden brown, tossing once or twice to ensure even toasting.
6. Take the hot, roasted pumpkin seeds out of the oven and allow them cool fully.
7. Give your guests the crunchy, flavorful Spicy Roasted Pumpkin Seeds to nibble on.

AVOCADO AND CRAB SALAD-STUFFED ENDIVE

Ingredients:
- 2 large endive heads
- 1 ripe avocado
- 4 ounces lump crab meat
- 1/4 cup diced red bell pepper
- 1/4 cup diced cucumber
- 1 tablespoon chopped fresh cilantro
- 1 tablespoon lime juice
- Salt and pepper to taste

Instructions:
1. Separate the leaves from each endive head by cutting off the base.
2. After rinsing, dry the endive leaves with a paper towel.
3. Use a fork to mash the avocado in a bowl to a smooth consistency.

4. Include the lump crab meat, lime juice, salt, pepper, cucumber, red bell pepper, and chopped fresh cilantro. Mix gently until thoroughly blended.
5. Fill each endive leaf with the avocado and crab salad.
6. Arrange the stuffed endive leaves with avocado and crab salad on a serving plate.
7. Offer the stuffed endive leaves as a classy and refreshing starter.

BAKED KALE CHIPS WITH NUTRITIONAL YEAST

Ingredients:
- 1 bunch, of kale, stems removed and leaves torn into bite-sized pieces
- 1 tablespoon olive oil
- 2 tablespoons nutritional yeast
- 1/2 teaspoon garlic powder
- 1/4 teaspoon salt (adjust to taste)

Instructions:
1. Set a baking sheet on your oven's 300°F (150°C) rack and preheat the oven.
2. Combine the kale leaves with salt, nutritional yeast, olive oil, and garlic powder in a large bowl. Make sure the coating covers the leaves uniformly.
3. Arrange the seasoned kale leaves in a single layer on the prepared baking sheet.
4. To ensure even cooking, turn the baking sheet halfway through baking and bake for 20 to 25 minutes or until the kale leaves are crispy and lightly browned.
5. Take the baked kale chips out of the oven and allow them to cool completely.
6. Offer your guests nutritional yeast-topped baked kale chips as a tasty and nutritious snack.

PROSCIUTTO-WRAPPED ASPARAGUS

Ingredients:
- Asparagus spears
- Thinly sliced prosciutto
- Olive oil
- Salt and pepper to taste

Instructions:
1. Set your oven to 400 degrees Fahrenheit (200 degrees Celsius) and cover a baking sheet with parchment paper.
2. Cut off the asparagus spears' rough ends.
3. Add salt and pepper to the asparagus spears and drizzle olive oil. Evenly coat by tossing.
4. Starting at the bottom and working your way up, tightly wrap a slice of prosciutto around each spear of asparagus.
5. Set the wrapped asparagus spears on the baking sheet that has been prepared.
6. Bake in the oven for 12 to 15 minutes or until the prosciutto is crisp and the asparagus is soft.
7. Take the prosciutto-wrapped asparagus out of the range and cool slightly before serving.
8. Offer the asparagus wrapped in prosciutto as a delectable and sophisticated starter or side dish.

MARINATED MOZZARELLA, CHERRY TOMATOES, AND OLIVES SKEWERS

Ingredients:
- Mozzarella balls (bocconcini)
- Cherry tomatoes
- Kalamata olives
- Fresh basil leaves
- Balsamic glaze
- Olive oil

- Salt and pepper to taste
- Wooden skewers

Instructions:

1. Thread a wooden skewer with a mozzarella ball, cherry tomato, Kalamata olive, and fresh basil leaf.
2. Carry on in this manner until you have the required quantity of skewers.
3. Position the skewers on a plate for serving.
4. Drizzle olive oil and balsamic glaze over the skewers.
5. To taste, add salt and pepper to the food.
6. As a tasty and eye-catching appetizer, serve the skewers of marinated mozzarella, cherry tomatoes, and olives.

CONCLUSION

In conclusion, adopting a low-carb, high-protein diet has become a well-liked strategy for enhancing general health, shedding pounds, and maintaining muscle mass. People who follow this diet, which emphasizes consuming lean meats, dairy, eggs, nuts, seeds, and green vegetables, report feeling fuller for extended periods and being less inclined to overeat and put on weight. A higher protein intake has also been associated with preserving and expanding lean body mass, which can boost metabolism and aid in weight management.

A low-carb, high-protein diet has also been found to provide several health advantages, including improved blood sugar regulation, a decreased risk of developing type 2 diabetes, and improved heart health. It has been demonstrated that cutting back on carbohydrates can improve insulin resistance and blood sugar levels, which lowers your risk of developing metabolic syndrome and its associated issues. By promoting the consumption of healthy fats and discouraging the consumption of processed and refined carbs, this eating pattern can also help to improve cholesterol profiles and general heart health.

The long-term health hazards of a low-carb, high-protein diet, such as kidney damage or inadequate nutritional intake, worry those who dislike it. But if the technology is utilized correctly and with the aid of a health worker, these potential issues can be minimized. To ensure they consume enough of the vitamins, minerals, and fiber they require, people following this diet should attempt to eat various nutrient-dense foods, such as vegetables, healthy fats, and high-quality protein sources.

Because every person has distinct dietary requirements and preferences, adopting a low-carb, high-protein diet is only a partial solution. However, this eating style has proven effective and sustainable for many people who desire to enhance their general well-being, control their weight, and improve their health. People considering this lifestyle change should speak with a qualified healthcare professional to see whether this approach suits their unique requirements and circumstances.

The low-carb, high-protein diet has ultimately demonstrated that it is a successful and healthful strategy for people to achieve their health and fitness goals. This diet reduces artificial carbs while emphasizing whole, nutrient-dense foods. This can aid in general health, weight loss, and satiety. As with any dietary adjustment, a unique and balanced approach, regular exercise, and regular check-ins with health professionals are the keys to long-term success and good health.

Printed in Great Britain
by Amazon

46250b1f-ac67-48e4-9129-4666f84b31c2R01